GUIDE TO THE
Amish Country

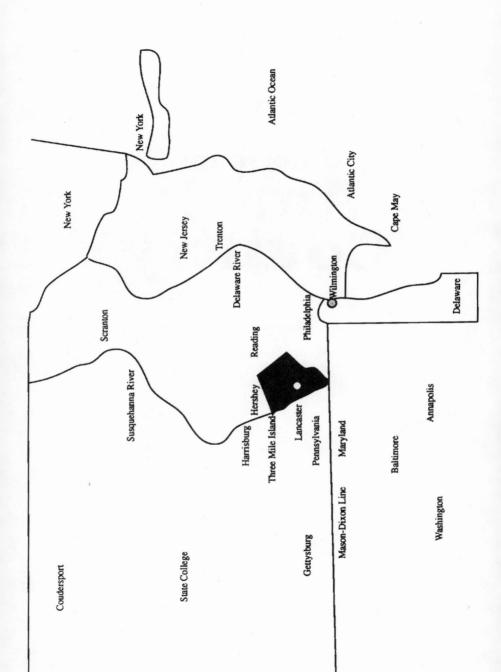

GUIDE TO THE
Amish
Country

by Bill Simpson

PELICAN PUBLISHING COMPANY
Gretna 1995

First edition, August 1992
Second edition, September 1995

*The word "Pelican" and the depiction of a pelican are trademarks
of Pelican Publishing Company, Inc.,
and are registered in the U.S. Patent and Trademark Office.*

Library of Congress Cataloging-in-Publication Data

Simpson, Bill, 1950-
    Guide to the Amish country / by Bill Simpson. — 2nd ed.
      p. cm.
    ISBN 1-56554-113-8 (pb : alk. paper)
    1. Amish Country (Pa.)—Guidebooks. I. Title.
F157.P44S56 1995
917.4804'43—dc20   95-16359
                                               CIP

Manufactured in the United States of America

Published by Pelican Publishing Company, Inc.
1101 Monroe Street, Gretna, Louisiana 70053

Contents

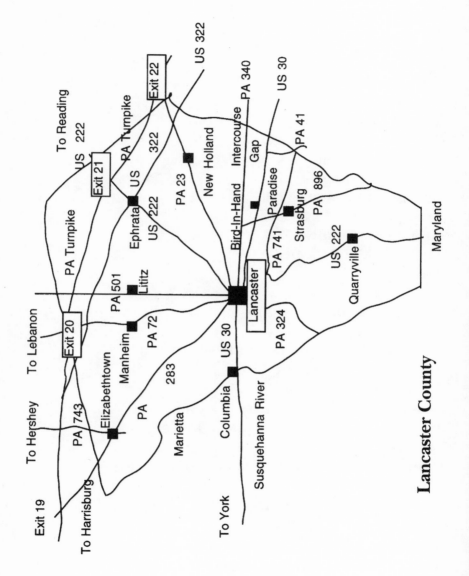

Lancaster County

Introduction

"Unique" is a strong and overused word, but it does describe the Amish Country. Of all the popular vacation destinations in North America, this section of Pennsylvania is the only one that's a farming area. It's also the only vacation destination whose primary attraction is a group of people—the Amish.

For those reasons, a visit to the Amish Country may be rather different from a vacation somewhere else. The Amish Country has no ocean or mountains, but it certainly has plenty of beautiful scenery. And, unlike the actors in many historical recreations, the Amish are real people leading their real lives. (See Visitor's Etiquette.)

If you've never been to the Amish Country, many aspects of it may surprise you—people travelling in horse-drawn buggies, farmers working their fields with horses, seemingly endless fields of corn, children going to school in one-room schoolhouses, covered bridges. What you'll find is that in many ways, the Amish live pretty much as they did 250 years ago.

You'll also find food, and plenty of it. Lancaster County is the most productive non-irrigated agricultural county in the U.S., producing more than half a billion dollars worth of agricultural commodities every year. A paradox is that much of that production comes from farmers who still use horse-drawn equipment.

Smorgasbords are a favorite local eating tradition. For one price, diners at a smorgasbord can eat all that they can hold. At roadside stands, farmers sell produce and baked goods directly to consumers.

The Amish Country has no exact geographic boundaries. Most Amish families in the area live in the eastern half of Lancaster County. Towns surrounded by Amish are Bird-In-Hand, Intercourse, New Holland, Strasburg, and Quarryville. On many roads in those areas, one Amish farm runs into another. There are also Amish families in neighboring counties, especially in western Chester County, near Honey Brook, and in southern Berks County, near Morgantown.

To get a real feel for the Amish Country, it's a good idea to get away from the busy main highways. A walk or a bike ride down a quiet country road will reveal sights that you'll never see from a car or a bus.

The real Amish Country is a land of country roads and small towns where neighbors know each other and where life moves at a comfortable pace. There's always work to be done, but there's always time to stop and chat too. It's a land where life still moves in rhythm with the changing seasons.

The best way to enjoy an Amish Country vacation is to relax. Find a quiet spot and watch the corn grow. Imagine that you have nowhere to go and all day to get there. Lancaster County has more miles of road than any other Pennsylvania county. Explore. You're sure to find something interesting, maybe even some things that you don't have at home.

GUIDE TO THE
Amish
Country

Cows.

An Amish farmer with his mules. Such sights are common along local country roads as spring field work progresses. (Courtesy Pennsylvania Dutch Visitors Bureau)

Visitor's Etiquette

The Amish appear to have a unique distinction, and it's one that doesn't especially thrill them. In all the world, they appear to be the only people who are a tourist attraction. The Amish Country has no ocean or mountains. Visitors come to see the Amish *people*. Because of this unique situation, it's extremely important for visitors to maintain standards of politeness and courtesy.

The Amish aren't actors. They're real people leading their real lives. The extensive tourist industry in Lancaster County has developed because of the Amish, but the Amish haven't promoted themselves. Instead, they've found themselves the objects of attention that they have trouble understanding.

A normal reaction of visitors first seeing the Amish is to have difficulty comprehending why people would choose to live without all the creature comforts that modern life can offer. However, that sense of curiosity generally changes to a sincere admiration for people who stick faithfully to their beliefs, people who don't base their lives on material success.

The Amish would probably prefer that visitors wouldn't come to look at them, but they've learned to live with the attention. In fact, they do benefit from the visitors' purchases of food, quilts, and other goods that they produce. Because of the tourists, Lancaster County Amish are relatively prosperous. That prosperity has little effect on their lives, however, because the Amish way of life does not encourage the pursuit of material wealth, or judge success by the number of goods a person acquires.

To put the tourist situation into perspective, simply think of how any other people would feel if a bus full of tourists armed with cameras pulled into their neighborhood, and the tour guide announced, "This is a Catholic (Jewish, Hindu, etc.) neighborhood, and this is how they live." Nobody would like that sort of treatment, but the Amish have 5,000,000 visitors come to look at them every year.

As long as visitors conduct themselves properly, they and the Amish can co-exist quite well. There have been many instances of visitors actually walking into Amish homes, taking pictures of them, and otherwise acting inconsiderately. Fortunately, those events seem to have decreased in recent years.

Here are some reminders for promoting good relationships between the Amish and visitors.

1. No trespassing. Remember that Amish homes, and schools, are private property. No one, whether Amish or not, would appreciate strangers walking around, taking pictures.

2. No pictures. For religious reasons, the Amish have been forbidden to have their pictures taken since early in the 20th century. They believe that a person who has his picture taken might become prideful, and their religion stresses the community over the individual.

With a camera, you'll create a sense of uneasiness in any Amish whom you may meet. If you do want to take pictures, shoot the fields and the animals.

3. Tread softly and drive slowly. If you find yourself behind a horse-drawn vehicle, remember that it's one of the reasons why you've chosen to visit this area, and think of the story that you'll have to tell your friends back home. An even better step is to park the car and travel by bicycle or on foot. You'll see and experience much more if you're not looking through windows. In general, cars and buggies don't mix well.

4. Don't bother to ask, "What's it like to be Amish?" It's the only life that they've ever known. They find modern life as puzzling as others find their lives.

The best way to get to talk to Amish people is to buy something from them, and to know something about what you are buying. For instance, if you know something about corn and tomatoes, you can stop at a roadside stand and carry on a good conversation about crops.

The Amish are generally very private but warm and friendly people. They won't normally initiate conversations with strangers. At their places of business, they'll answer your questions helpfully, but they'll never give you a sales pitch.

The best rule is simply to treat the Amish, and everybody else, with respect.

An Amish boy plowing with a four-horse team. (Courtesy Pennsylvania Dutch Visitors Bureau)

Who Are the Amish?

The Amish are a Christian sect. Their interpretations of the Bible and their faith in God are the guiding forces in their lives. They choose not to use many modern conveniences, such as cars and electricity, because they believe that worldliness drives a wedge between man and God.

The Amish are one of three Anabaptist sects in Lancaster County. The others are Mennonites and Brethren. These religions don't baptize children into the faith. Rather, adults choose to join or not to join the church when they're old enough to make their own decisions.

The Amish sect had its beginnings in Switzerland in 1693 when a Mennonite bishop named Jacob Amman broke away from his brethren and formed a new fellowship. In the 1700s, they emigrated to the United States to escape religious persecution.

The first Amish settlement in the United States was in Lancaster County. They chose the area because its rich limestone soil and abundant water were ideal for farming, their primary occupation. Throughout their entire history, the Amish have been an agrarian society. Today, farming is still their primary occupation, but not their only one.

From Lancaster County, some Amish moved on and established new communities. Today, Amish live in 20 states and in Ontario, Canada. Many Pennsylvania counties have Amish populations, but more than 50 percent of Pennsylvania's Amish, approximately 17,000 people, live in Lancaster County. Some also live in neighboring Chester, Berks, York, and Lebanon counties. Other Pennsylvania Amish communities are in Union and Snyder counties, Mifflin County, Centre County, Montour County, and Mercer County.

What's the Attraction of the Amish?

In a world where everything seems to move at 100 MPH, a place where life still moves slowly holds a special attraction, and life in the Amish Country still moves at its own pace. Horse-drawn buggies generally move along at 10-12 MPH. Crops grow slowly. On the farm, there's always work to be done, but there are no time clocks. For a visitor, it's nice to fantasize about leading such a life.

Visitors also enjoy looking at a culture that has held together for centuries, and that still embraces values that are frequently called "old-fashioned." Amish life revolves around God, family, community, the soil, and hard work.

It's easy to look at the Amish and to see their lifestyle as one of deprivation, but they don't see themselves that way. The focus of their lives isn't what they don't have, but what they do have. In their view, their values are superior to materialistic values. That's why they continue to live as they do.

Amish life is by no means perfect, nor is it as idyllic as it may appear. They're human and they face the same trials and challenges as everyone else confronts. They have bills to pay and children to rear. They get sick just like everyone else. And, they face certain situations that confront them simply because they're Amish. Travelling in buggies on busy highways can be tough. Being the object of tourists' curiosity can be unsettling.

Today, the Amish are facing problems caused by increasing population, both their own and the world in general. The Amish population is burgeoning. More than 50 percent of all Amish are under 18 years of age, and the growth pressures from outside are making farms more valuable for housing developments than for farming. As a result, many Amish are being forced into nonfarm occupations. In a perfect world, all Amish would be farmers. But, there simply aren't enough farms to go around.

Still, the Amish persevere and thrive. They have extended, loving families in which everyone has a place of respect and importance. They have no retirement homes. Instead, if the elderly need assistance, their children care for them. And, not having televisions and radios has advantages. The Amish don't know the problems of everyone on earth. While it's true that they don't embrace the latest technological marvels, they also don't suffer such modern scourges as poverty, broken homes, drugs, etc.

For the Amish, life still moves in harmony with the seasons. While modern life has been reduced to two seasons—50 weeks of work and two weeks of vacation—farm life still has four distinct seasons. Spring is for planting, summer is for growing, autumn is for harvesting, and winter is for preparing for spring. For the Amish, there's a fifth season: Wedding Season. Amish weddings traditionally take place in November and early December, after the harvest is complete.

Amish children go to school for eight years. In Pennsylvania, the Amish operate their own school system. Almost always, the schools have only one room, and all eight grades have the same teacher.

Until the 1930s, all Pennsylvania Amish attended public schools. The break began when the public schools started to promote consolidations and bussing. The Amish wanted to keep their children within walking distance of school, so they began their own school system. Today, there are more than 150 one-room schools in the area, and new ones are still being built. Amish schools teach the basics, but have no formal religion classes. Teaching religion is a family responsibility. Amish schools do, however, have Bible readings, prayers, and hymn sings. The schools foster a sense of community, not of competition. Their purpose is to train children to be members of the Amish community, not to be engineers and lawyers.

Parents are in charge of the schools. The school board, all male, meets monthly with the teachers. Parents are always welcome at school, and often drop by to visit. Fathers repair the buildings; mothers bring surprise hot meals during winter.

A typical farm scene.

Common Questions about the Amish

Q. Why don't the Amish use cars?

A. The Amish believe that cars pull people apart, and that a car distorts its owner's sense of self-importance in a world where humility is a necessary virtue. Besides, they haven't adopted the belief that faster is automatically better. The Amish don't, however, believe that the internal combustion engine is inherently evil. They do hire drivers to transport them. Their primary aversion to cars is their belief that cars pull families apart.

Q. Are the Amish all the same?

A. No. Like everyone else, they're individuals. All groups of Amish don't have exactly the same beliefs and customs, either. Some church districts are much more conservative than others. The Amish in Lancaster and Chester counties are generally considered rather conservative.

Q. Does anyone ever join the Amish?

A. It's rare. Amish life frequently looks inviting, but most modern Americans wouldn't actually be willing to give up the lives, and the material goods, that they know.

Q. Do Amish ever leave their culture?

A. Yes, but about 80 percent choose to stay, and many who do leave eventually return. An Amish upbringing doesn't do a good job of preparing someone for life in the outside or "English" world. Going from an environment that stresses spiritual values to a materialistic environment isn't easy.

Q. Do Amish ever go to hospitals?

A. Yes, although they prefer not to. Most Amish births take place at home, normally with the assistance of a midwife.

Q. Do the Amish make much money?

A. They generally make a comfortable living, and they own valuable real estate, but the attainment of wealth has no importance in their culture. A millionaire couldn't display his wealth without offending his community.

Q. Is food a part of their religion?

A. No. But it's a part of their culture, just as it's a part of just about every culture on earth. They have favorite dishes, many of which are common to a specific area, such as shoo-fly pie.

Q. Is the Amish community growing?

A. Yes. For instance, in the past 25 years, the Amish population in Lancaster County has just about doubled.

Q. Are all Amish farmers?

A. No. Some work in trades such as furniture making, and in retail businesses. Much of the equipment that they use must be modified before they can use it, because no one manufactures horse-drawn farm machinery any longer. The market is simply too small. This provides many job opportunities. Many Amish women engage in quilt making. Even the Amish who don't actually operate a farm, however, are certain to maintain a large garden.

Q. Do Amish people dislike tourists?

A. It might be more accurate to say that they dislike cameras, and the intrusions that tourists can make into their lives. The Amish have become accustomed to visitors, and they even profit from selling produce and goods. Still, they're private people and it's important for visitors to respect that privacy.

Q. Are the Amish really different from everyone else?

A. No. Like everyone else, they're searching for happiness and contentment in this life.

A. Yes. They're also preparing themselves for eternal life, and they believe that preparation dictates how they live.

A. No. They pay taxes just as everyone else does.

A. Yes. They're not a mobile society. They'll frequently grow up, marry, raise a family, grow old, and die all within a few miles of where they were born, perhaps on the same farm. When Amish families do move, it's never just one family. They need enough people to form a small settlement, perhaps half a dozen families.

Amish farmhouses.

There are no easy, simple answers to the questions about Amish life. In some ways, they're like everyone everywhere. In other ways, they're completely different. Still, it's not especially hard to understand why visitors find the Amish so fascinating.

In a world where most families never sit down at the dinner table together, it's reassuring to see three or four generations of one family working together in the fields. In a world where things change overnight, it's reassuring to see a culture where change comes slowly, if it ever comes. In a world that worships bigness, it's reassuring to see the small, efficient, meticulous farms of the Amish.

About 250 years ago, the Amish didn't have any particular appeal—everybody travelled by horse and buggy. About 100 years ago, that was still true. Today, of course, the Amish are a distinct minority. They've stayed where they were while the world has gone zooming by. Their lives were never broken, so they didn't attempt to fix them.

No one will claim that Amish life is perfect, but if you judge it by the smiles on the faces of children walking home from school, then it's certainly a pretty good way to live.

Old Order Mennonites

The Amish aren't the only horse and buggy sect in the area. The Old Order Mennonites parallel the Amish in their beliefs and customs. In fact, in many ways, Old Order Mennonites are more conservative than the Amish.

The Old Order Mennonite community is centered around Terre Hill and Martindale in northeastern Lancaster County. On a Sunday morning, the roads are filled with bicycles carrying Mennonite men and women to church.

One minor difference between the Amish and the Old Order Mennonites is that the Mennonites have churches, or meeting-houses, while the Amish conduct their worship services in their homes.

Like the Amish, the Old Order Mennonites are primarily farmers.

Not all Mennonites lead the conservative, rural life.

Mennonite churches are in big cities and small towns all over the world. Mennonites are active missionaries, especially in Africa and Latin America.

Despite the obstacles that they face, the Amish are thriving today. The year 1993 marked the 300th birthday of Amish society. As recently as 1900, they numbered only 5,000. Today, their numbers are above 100,000 in North America.

For more detailed looks into Amish life, two of the best books are:

The Riddle of Amish Culture, Donald B. Kraybill, Johns Hopkins University Press

Amish Society, John A. Hostetler, Johns Hopkins University Press

The Amish Country Yesterday

Although southeastern Pennsylvania developed as an agricultural area, and gained a reputation as the home of the Pennsylvania Dutch, not everyone was a farmer, and not everyone was Pennsylvania Dutch. Immigrants from many places and believers of many faiths learned to live together. This mixture of people produced a middle class that possessed an enviable assortment of mechanical and intellectual skills, as well as a powerful work ethic.

The earliest permanent settlers in Lancaster County were a group of Swiss Mennonites. They believed in complete separation of church and state and came to Pennsylvania in search of religious freedom. The fertile farmlands along the Pequea (PECK-way) Creek reminded them of Palatinate Germany, and many families moved to Lancaster County in the early 18th century. The Amish followed, with their first wave arriving between 1737 and 1754.

Many other groups also came in search of religious freedom. Among them were the French Huguenots, the Quakers, and the Scotch-Irish. Despite their many differences, they managed to co-exist fairly peacefully.

Lancaster County was formed from part of Chester County in 1729. At the time, it was much larger than it is today. Eventually, parts of Lancaster County became York, Cumberland, Northumberland, Berks, Dauphin, and Lebanon counties. The boundaries have been the same since 1813. Lancaster County now covers an area of 946 square miles. It's almost the size of Rhode Island.

While farmers worked the area's lush fields, forges nearby produced iron to build the new nation. During the French and Indian wars, and the Revolutionary War, Lancaster County supplied the nation with both guns and butter.

Throughout the area, place names give evidence of the importance of the iron industry. Martic Forge, Speedwell Forge, Hopewell Furnace, Pool Forge, and Windsor Forge were iron-making sites. Cornwall Banks in Lebanon County held the largest deposit of iron ore east of Lake Superior and was operated for more than two centuries.

When George Washington was elected president in 1789, Gen. Edward Hand of Lancaster, Washington's adjutant general, suggested that Lancaster would be a good capital for the new nation. Among Lancaster's qualifications was a population of 4,200, making it the largest inland city in the United States. It also boasted industries such as 14 hatters, 36 shoemakers, 25 tailors, 7 gunsmiths, and 3 printing presses. Lancaster also was home to 40 public buildings, or taverns. Lancaster had been the capital for a day, September 27, 1777, when Congress fled from Philadelphia, but it never became the permanent capital.

The first turnpike in the United States ran from Philadelphia to Lancaster. Begun in 1792 and opened in 1794, it was a toll road with hard-surfaced tracks for wagon wheels, a significant improvement over the dirt roads that were standard everywhere else. Along its route were 62 taverns.

Farmers grew large quantities of grain, and scores of mills along Lancaster County's streams ground flour for shipment to Philadelphia and Baltimore. Place names reflect the presence of many mills—Mill Creek, Millway, Millport, Kramer Mill Road, Lewis Mills Road.

With so much grain available, the area became a major producer of beer. For a time, a malthouse in the small borough of Mount Joy in Lancaster County claimed to be the "Malt Capital of the Nation." That claim was debatable. Certainly, the competition was fierce.

By the 1840s, tobacco had become an important crop in Lancaster County. Tobacco growing and cigar manufacturing became fairly significant parts of the local economy.

Lancaster County was a major transportation center, and the famous Conestoga wagons were developed and built here. Many of their design features were different from other wagons. Probably the most distinctive feature of the Conestoga wagons was the "lazy board" on which the driver sat. It extended out from the left side of the wagon, and enabled him to apply the hand brake, and to ride astride the wheelhorse. This probably led to the American custom of driving on the right side of the road, with the driver on the left.

The location of Lancaster and Chester counties on the Maryland border made them important stops for runaway slaves on the Underground Railroad. Many slaves hid in barns and cellars on their way to freedom. A riot at Christiana in 1851 was one of the earliest cases of citizens' anger with the Fugitive Slave Law.

Throughout the 19th century, the area grew. Industries developed, but agriculture remained dominant. In 1907, a major event in Lancaster's history occurred. It was then that Armstrong Cork Company chose 50 acres beside the railroad tracks as the site for its new linoleum manufacturing facility. Eventually, it became the biggest producer of linoleum in the world, as well as Lancaster's biggest employer.

Only in the last half-century have the Amish become famous. When everyone travelled in buggies, they didn't stand out. However, as the rest of the world has embraced new technology, the Amish have gained fame by maintaining their old ways. Lancaster County's tourist industry didn't become an important part of the local economy until the mid-1950s.

Contrasts of culture abound in the Amish Country. Moving day for an Amish family, for example, means loading household possessions on a mule-drawn wagon, while an airplane on the horizon provides other residents with a much different mode of travel. (Courtesy Pennsylvania Visitors Bureau)

Sledders hitch a ride behind a mule-drawn sleigh. Off-road transportation is a common way to get around for the Amish. (Courtesy Pennsylvania Dutch Visitors Bureau)

The Amish Country Today

A modern office complex sitting beside a farm where horses and windmills still provide the power is a good example of the diversity evident in the Amish Country today. While the world around them races along, the Amish still do things the way they've always done them, and at their own pace. Traffic frequently slows to a crawl behind a buggy. Amish women still give birth at home, with the help of midwives. Entire families work the fields together. God, family, and hard work are still the important factors in Amish life. The attainment of material wealth is not an acceptable goal for the Amish. They aren't interested in making lots of money and retiring early.

The Amish are actually a small minority, and the rest of the population of the Amish Country drives cars and leads fairly typical American lives. The economy is diversified, featuring agriculture, manufacturing, services, and tourism.

In contrast to much of Pennsylvania, the Amish Country is a growing area. The Amish population is burgeoning, and many outsiders are moving to Lancaster and surrounding counties.

For decades, unchecked growth was welcomed as a sign of prosperity. In recent years, attitudes have changed. Today, any developer who proposes a new housing community or shopping center can expect a major battle before his plans win approval, if they ever win approval. Agricultural preservation movements are fighting the loss of farmland, with moderately good success. Many farmers have sold their development rights, guaranteeing that their farms will remain farms forever. One such farm was the setting for the movie *Witness*.

Despite the encroachment of development, the Amish Country still has a distinctly rural flavor. It's possible to ride a bike for miles and see almost nothing but farms. Agricultural fairs are still major social events in many towns. Farmer's markets bring food from the farm directly to buyers. Agricultural businesses employ thousands of local residents. Despite the loss of many farms, Lancaster County has more than twice the agricultural production of any other county in Pennsylvania.

For the Amish, these are times that test their values. In previous years, an Amish father would buy a farm for each of his sons when the son was old enough to leave home. Today, that happens much less frequently. The reasons are many. One is the high price of farms. When housing developers and farmers get into a bidding war, the developer usually has the deeper pockets. Another reason is that all of the available land is in farming. Even without competition from developers, the Amish would have trouble finding enough farms. Their population has about doubled in the past 25 years, but the amount of land has remained constant.

Faced with this dilemma, many Amish are choosing nonfarming jobs. They're doing quite well in many different businesses, and by working in nonfarm occupations, they're able to stay in the area. Amish families are also buying farms in areas of Lancaster County where they haven't traditionally lived.

Faced with the same problem, many Old Order Mennonite families are taking a different approach. They're moving out of the area and establishing new communities in other areas of Pennsylvania, and in other states. To the Amish, staying close to family is most important. To the Old Order Mennonites, staying in farming is most important.

For everyone in the Amish Country, this is a time of decisions. Philadelphia is pushing westward. Without proper planning, the megalopolis could swallow up Chester and Lancaster counties. Many people don't want to see that happen, and they're fighting to preserve the Amish Country's rural heritage.

the Amish are beginning to speak out. In recent years, they've turned up at public meetings to voice their disapproval of highways and developments that would gobble up hundreds of acres of productive farmland, and cause them other hardships.

The Amish have even hinted that they might move en masse, but that's unlikely. They don't want to move. This is their home, and it has been their home for hundreds of years. Lancaster County's fine soil makes farming comparatively easy. There are no guarantees, but the Amish are likely to be here for a while. *They* aren't selling farms to turn a quick buck.

If you want to know more about farmland preservation efforts, and if you'd like to contribute to the cause, contact: Lancaster Farmland Trust, 128 E. Marion Street, Lancaster, PA 17602. Phone 717-293-0707.

Facts and Figures

Where Is It? While Amish people live in 20 states and Canada, the best-known Amish area is in southeastern Pennsylvania. Most of the Amish in this area live in Lancaster County. Some also live in neighboring Chester, Lebanon, Berks, and York counties. The Amish Country is about 55 miles west of Philadelphia. The line of 40⁰ North latitude passes through southern York, Lancaster, and Chester counties, about 15 miles north of the Mason-Dixon Line, Pennsylvania's border with Maryland.

What's to See and Do: There are enough attractions, historic sights, shopping opportunities, recreational activities, and eating establishments to keep a visitor busy for a day or a fortnight. Almost all of the Amish-related attractions are in Lancaster County.

A broader area of southeastern Pennsylvania is known as Pennsylvania Dutch Country. There are no exact geographic definitions, but it extends roughly from the Brandywine Creek in Chester County, west to Chambersburg, and north to Lewisburg.

Pennsylvania Dutch is both a culture and a language. The culture encompasses people of many religions, with Amish and Mennonites being the most widely known. A slogan on T-shirts says, "If you ain't Dutch, you ain't much." The language is widely spoken by the Amish and Mennonites. It's a mix of German and English. If you happen to hear people speaking a language that you don't recognize, it's probably Pennsylvania Dutch. Actually, the Pennsylvania Dutch are of German ancestry. Dutch is a derivation of the German *Deutsche.*

The Land: The Amish Country became the Amish Country because of its rich limestone soil. Early Amish immigrants to the new world decided to settle here because the good earth was ideal for farming, their primary occupation. Their hard work and that rich earth have combined to make Lancaster County the most productive non-irrigated agricultural county in the United States.

Most of the area is rolling hills. The areas along the Susquehanna River have fairly rugged hills. The Welsh Mountains in eastern Lancaster County are actually steep hills.

Many streams meander through the Dutch Country. The Susquehanna River is easily the biggest. The Schuylkill River is also a major waterway. The Conestoga River is the major river in the heart of Lancaster County's Amish Country.

The Climate: The climate has four distinct seasons and overall, it's rather mild. (See Planning Your Visit.) For local weather reports, you can call the weather center at Millersville University, 717-872-3692.

Emergency Services: Dial 911 for police, ambulance, and fire services.

Hospitals:

Brandywine Hospital, Coatesville, 215-383-8124

Columbia Hospital, 631 Poplar Street, 717-684-2841

Community Hospital of Lancaster, 1100 E. Orange Street, 717-397-3711

Ephrata Community Hospital, Martin Avenue, 717-733-0311

Harrisburg Hospital, S. Front Street, 717-782-3131

Hershey Medical Center, 500 University Drive, 717-531-8333

Lancaster General Hospital, 555 H. Duke Street, Lancaster, 717-299-5511

Reading Hospital, Sixth and Spruce streets, West Reading, 215-378-6218

Saint Joseph Hospital, 250 College Avenue, Lancaster, 717-291-8211

Periodicals: Many periodicals cover events and offer calen-

tors bureaus and in most establishments. You can also order them through the mail.

Amish Country News, P.O. Box 497, Intercourse, PA 17534. Six issues for $7.

Intercourse News, P.O. Box 373, Intercourse, PA 17534. Twelve issues for $15.

PennDutch Traveler, 408 N. Market Street, Lancaster, PA 17603. Sixteen issues for $12.

This Month Magazine, P.O. Box 3645, Harrisburg, PA 17105-3645. Yearly subscription is $15; $1.50 for single copy.

Local newspapers are the Lancaster *Intelligencer Journal* (morning) and the *Lancaster New Era* (evening and Sunday). These carry listings of events and are available throughout Lancaster County. The offices are at 8 W. King Street in downtown Lancaster. In addition, many small towns have weekly newspapers.

Radio Stations: When you're in the Amish Country, you can generally pick up any local stations during the day. At night, reception improves greatly. If you're a baseball fan, you can follow all the Orioles and Phillies games. At night, you can usually pick up the Yankees, Red Sox, Tigers, Indians, Mets, Cardinals, and Reds. If you don't mind a little static, you can hear the Cubs, White Sox, Pirates, Blue Jays, Rangers, and Twins.

Local Stations:
WSBA—910 AM (Talk, Orioles)
WLAN—1390 AM (Mellow music)
WCOJ—1420 AM (Contemporary)
WLPA—1490 AM (News, Phillies and Orioles)
WITF—88.5 FM (Public Radio)
WFNM—89.1 FM (College variety, mostly Rock)
WJTL—90.3 FM (Contemporary Christian)
WCTX—91.3 FM (Spanish language)
WIXQ—91.7 FM (College Variety, mostly Rock)
WIOV—105.1 FM (Country)
Baseball:
Orioles—910 AM, 1090 AM, 1490 AM

Phillies—850 AM, 1210 AM, 1270 AM, 1490 AM
Local Television:
WGAL—Channel 8 (NBC)
WLYH—Channel 15 (CBS)
WHP—Channel 21 (CBS)
WHTM—Channel 27 (ABC)
WITF—Channel 33 (PBS)
WPMT—Channel 43 (Fox)
Visitors Information Centers:
Chester County Tourist Bureau, 117 W. Gay Street, West Chester, PA 19380. Phone 215-344-6365.

Downtown Visitors Center, 100 S. Queen Street, Southern Market Center, Lancaster. Open Monday-Friday 8:30 to 5, Saturday 9 to 4, Sunday 11 to 3. Phone 397-3531.

Gettysburg Travel Council, 35 Carlisle Street, Gettysburg, PA 17325. Phone 717-334-6274.

Harrisburg-Hershey-Carlisle Tourism & Convention Bureau, 114 Walnut Street, Box 969, Harrisburg, PA 17108. Phone 717-232-1377.

Hershey Information, 300 Park Boulevard, Hershey, PA 17033. Phone 800-HERSHEY.

Intercourse Information Center, Route 340, Intercourse. Open Monday-Saturday 9:30 to 5, Sunday noon to 5. Phone 768-3882.

Lebanon Valley Tourist & Visitors Bureau, P.O. Box 626, Lebanon, PA 17042. Phone 717-272-8555.

Mennonite Information Center, Millstream Road and Route 30, east of Lancaster. Open Monday-Saturday 8-5. Phone 299-0954.

Pennsylvania Dutch Visitors Bureau, 501 Greenfield Road, Lancaster. Exit Route 30 Bypass east of Lancaster. Open Sunday-Thursday 8 to 6, Friday-Saturday 8 to 7. Phone 299-8901.

Susquehanna Heritage & Tourist Information Center, Linden Street between Third and Fifth, Columbia. Open daily 9 to 4. Phone 717-684-2199.

York County Convention & Visitors Bureau, One Market Way East, P.O. Box 1229, York, PA 17405. Phone 717-848-4000.

Quick Facts:

Time Zone: Eastern

Alcoholic Beverages: Twenty-one is minimum age for purchase and consumption. No alcohol may be brought in from other states. Taverns and distributors sell beer. Liquor is available only through state stores.

Minimum age for drivers: 16

Legal Holidays: January 1, Martin Luther King's Birthday (third Monday in January), President's Day (third Monday in February), Memorial Day (last Monday in May), July 4, Labor Day (first Monday in September), Columbus Day (second Monday in October), Veterans Day (November 11), Thanksgiving (fourth Thursday in November), Christmas. Note: Amish do not celebrate secular holidays, only religious ones.

Planning Your Visit

Here are some tips for enjoying your stay in the Amish Country.

First, it's good to make reservations whenever you come. The "No Vacancy" signs go on frequently, even at unexpected times, such as President's Day weekend in February. If you show up without reservations, you have a good chance of having a difficult time finding a place to stay.

How expensive the Amish Country accommodations seem will depend on where you're coming from. If you're accustomed to Manhattan prices for hotels and restaurants, the Amish Country will look like a real bargain. Otherwise, it will appear fairly average. And, there are many places where you can get good prices on all sorts of items.

A typical vacation in the Amish Country is rather leisurely. It's more watching and looking than participating. Visitors come for many reasons. Some of the major ones are: to get a glimpse of a different culture, to relax, to see historic sites, and to eat.

Food is a major attraction of the Amish Country. Pennsylvania Dutch food is traditionally fresh and simple, featuring many items straight from the farm. It's also quite plentiful. A favorite eating experience is a trip to a smorgasbord, a restaurant where you can eat as much as you can hold for one price.

What to Wear: Casual attire is the norm. Unless you're going to the theater, to church, or to a fancy restaurant, there's no need to put on a coat and tie or a dress. This is a rather conservative area, however, so overly skimpy outfits are likely to draw stares of disapproval.

When to Come: Summer is the biggest season for visitors, but people find plenty of reasons to come all year. Autumn is harvest time, and generally the driest time of the year. Spring is planting time and the earth is beautiful and colorful. Winter is quiet and relaxed.

Some attractions are closed in winter, so that may be a consideration in planning your trip, but there's always plenty to see and eat. The Amish Country isn't a beach resort. Life goes on all year.

The Weather: The Amish Country has a temperate climate, with four distinct seasons. The climate is similar to that of all the big cities of the East Coast. Spring is very changeable. It can go from cool and rainy to dry and warm overnight. Normally, spring is the rainiest season. If you come then, you'll want to bring clothes for warm weather, and for cool weather.

Summer is pretty hot most of the time. Temperatures get to 100 degrees F a few times every summer. Most summer rain comes from thunderstorms. They can be intense and dangerous, but they usually don't last long. For a summer visit, a light jacket will be sufficient, and you'll probably never need it.

Autumn can be rather spectacular. Temperatures are pleasant and humidity is low. Occasionally, snow will show up in October, but it's more common to get into November without a hard frost than to have snow before Halloween. In autumn, temperatures change fairly significantly from morning to afternoon. It can be 40 degrees at sunrise and 70 or 75 in the middle of the day.

Until 1994, winters had been in a mild pattern. Through January, February, and March of 1994, bitter cold and frequent storms made the East Coast an icy wasteland. Of course, no one can predict whether that year was just an aberration, or the beginning of a series of bad winters. Before 1994, snowfall had declined in recent years. In the winter of 1990-91, for instance, a storm shortly after Christmas dropped 10 inches of snow, but that was about it for the entire season. There were several other nuisance snows, but that was the only one of any stature. That year, the lowest temperature in Lancaster was 10 degrees F. In 1994, the mercury sank to -19 F, and schools were shut for a week. But 1994-95 was as mild as 1993-94 was harsh, so it's difficult to say what a typical winter in the Amish Country is.

Getting Here: The Amish Country is close to many of the major population centers of the East Coast. Here are some highway mileages from Lancaster:

Baltimore   67
Boston   359
Charlotte   540
Cincinnati   560
Montreal   525
New York   160
Philadelphia   65
Pittsburgh   225
Richmond   212
Toronto   465
Washington   110

For millions of people, the Amish Country is an easy drive or train ride away. If you live in New York, Philadelphia, Baltimore, or Washington, the Amish Country is ideal for a weekend vacation, or even for a day trip.

Avoiding Traffic Jams: If traffic bothers you, there are certain places to avoid at certain times. Summer is most crowded, and weekends are more crowded than weekdays. Most of the traffic stays on the major highways. Route 741 in Strasburg can look like the Long Island Expressway on a summer Saturday afternoon. Route 30 outside Lancaster can also get pretty crowded, as can Route 340 in Intercourse. But, if you come on a Tuesday afternoon in December, the going will be much easier. Autumn is actually a very popular time to visit, and crowds can be pretty thick then, especially on beautiful weekends.

Things to Bring: The main thing that will come in handy is a good map. Roads in the Amish Country rarely run at 90-degree angles. They follow streams and hills. It's easy to find yourself heading south when you think you're going east. Most convenience stores in the area have a good selection of maps.

ATM Machines: Banks and some convenience stores offer service from ATM machines.

Automobile Club—American Automobile Association:

Gettysburg—19 Lincoln Square, 717-334-1155

Harrisburg—2023 King Boulevard, 717-236-4021

Hershey—11 Briarcrest Square, 717-533-3381

Lancaster—34 N. Prince Street, 717-397-4444

              804 Estelle Drive, 717-898-6900

Lititz—118 W. Airport Road, 717-560-1706

West Chester—844 Paoli Pike, 215-696-8100

York—118 E. Market Street, 717-845-7676

Suggested Itinerary

For most visitors, a visit to the Amish Country provides a look at a different culture. The first thing that many people want to see is a horse and buggy. Since they're the Amish people's primary mode of transportation, and there are about 20,000 Amish in the area, buggies are pretty easy to spot. If you drive down Route 340, you're almost certain to get into traffic behind one.

After spotting a buggy, food is usually everybody's priority. It's not hard to find. Food of just about every description is readily available in the Amish Country. In restaurants, snack shops, and at roadside stands, there's food for every hunger.

If you have plenty of time, it's possible to see a large number of sights and attractions. But, if you have limited time, such as a three-day weekend, then you'll want to make the most of the available time. Here's a suggested itinerary that will take you to a variety of places, giving you a look at Amish life and history. It will take you through covered bridges, to a big outdoor market, for a train ride, and to several museums.

Friday: First stop is the **Green Dragon Market** on North State Street in Ephrata. The Green Dragon is an excellent place to buy just about everything, especially food. It's part farmer's market, part flea market. Fresh produce, baked goods, french fries, pretzels, funnel cakes, ice cream, and pizza are some of the things you can consume here. You can also buy watches,

The Old Order Amish rely on the horse and buggy for their transportation needs. After a day of shopping, father and son head home from Zimmerman's Hardware Store in Intercourse. (Courtesy Pennsylvania Dutch Visitors Bureau)

clothes, crafts, and just about everything except cars and houses.

Amish merchants man many of the stands here. Frequently, there's also a hay auction. Dozens of trucks loaded with straw and hay show up and farmers bid on the loads. It's easy to spend a few hours at the Green Dragon.

From the Green Dragon, you can begin a tour of the Amish Country's **covered bridges** (see "Self-Guided Tours"). On this tour, you'll see Amish farms and shops. Afterwards, you'll probably be ready for food and rest.

Saturday: Saturday's activities begin with another tour. This is the **"Heart of the Amish Country"** (see "Self-Guided Tours"). If you've brought the bicycles, this is an excellent ride.

After the tour, the next stop is the **People's Place** in Intercourse. There, you can learn a lot about Amish and Mennonite history and culture. At adjacent **Kitchen Kettle Village,** you can do some shopping and eating. If you want to take home any items from roadside stands, you'll have to buy them on Saturday. Almost all are closed on Sunday.

If you're interested in shopping, the **outlet centers** on Route 30 are open until 9 on Saturday nights.

Sunday: For Mennonite and Amish families, Sunday begins with **church services.** Many churches in the area have signs encouraging visitors to join them. Don't look for Amish churches, though. The Amish worship in their homes. There are, however, several Amish/Mennonite churches. One is at the intersection of Church and Orchard roads, just north of Route 340 in Bird-In-Hand. Another is on Mine Road, just south of Route 741 in Gap.

For **bicycling** enthusiasts, Sunday mornings are a great time to ride. Traffic is minimal. If you ride in the Terre Hill/Martindale area of northeastern Lancaster County on a Sunday morning, you'll share the roads with many Mennonite bicyclists who are pedaling to church.

Sunday brunch is a popular meal at many restaurants, but not at all of them. Some are closed on Sunday.

The **Strasburg Railroad** is open on Sundays, and a ride on the rails provides a different look at the area's fertile farmlands. After riding the rails, you can walk across the street and see the history of trains at the **Railroad Museum of Pennsylvania,** which underwent a major expansion in 1994.

By then, it will be Sunday afternoon, time to think about a big meal and the trip home. In three days, you won't have seen everything, but you should have gotten a bit of a feel for the Amish Country.

The Opposite Approach: It's not really necessary to lay out an itinerary. Improvising can be just as much fun.

Day by Day

One factor to keep in mind when you visit the Amish Country is that many of the attractions and shops are not open seven days a week. One of the most common signs that you'll see is *No Sunday Sales*. Sundays belong to God and family. This sign appears on just about every home-based business and roadside stand. So, if you're coming for a weekend and you want to load up with fresh produce or baked goods, buy on Saturday. It's also pretty tough to buy a quilt on Sunday.

This doesn't mean that the entire area shuts down on Sundays. All of the major businesses and restaurants are open, but you can't get much of anything directly from the farm.

Many other operations are open one, two, or three days a week. Farmers' markets are usually open two or three days. Central Market in Lancaster is open Tuesdays, Fridays, and Saturdays. The Bird-In-Hand Farmer's Market is open Friday and Saturday all year, and Wednesday (April-November) and Thursday (July-October). The Green Dragon Market is open only on Fridays. Root's Country Market is open only on Tuesdays. Renninger's Antique Market operates on Sundays.

To avoid disappointment, check the days (and months) of operation of the places that you intend to visit.

Names

If you look at a map of the Amish Country, you'll notice some rather interesting names. In the heart of Amish Country, it's just a few miles from Bird-In-Hand to Blue Ball to Intercourse to Paradise. On some maps, you'll find a place called Fertility. Where did these names come from?

Bird-In-Hand and Blue Ball took their names from tavern signs. When the area was first settled, much of the population was illiterate. People couldn't read signs, but they could recognize things. Thus, every tavern had a distinctive sign, such as a man with a bird in hand, and a blue ball.

The origin of the name *Intercourse* is less certain. At one time, the village was Cross Keys. One theory is that there was a race-course in the area with a sign that said *Enter Course*. This may have become *Intercourse*.

Paradise supposedly received its name from Joshua Scott, a famous local cartographer, who remarked, "This place should be called Paradise." If Paradise is green and fertile, the name seems appropriate.

Many other names have more obvious origins. The name *Lancaster* comes from Lancashire in England, which was the original home of John Wright, an early and prominent settler. Quarryville was home to many quarries. Willow Street had many willow trees. A logical question of East Petersburg is, "East of what?" Actually, it's east of Petersburg, which is in the central part of Pennsylvania. When the original settlers were naming it, they discovered that there already was a Petersburg in the state, so they made their new village East Petersburg.

Many road names tell you what you'll find on them. Go down Brick Church Road and you'll see a brick church. Turn onto Covered Bridge Road and you'll come to a covered bridge. Haiti Road, however, won't take you to Haiti. You may also notice that several roads in the area have the same name, such as Covered Bridge Road, and White Oak Road.

Among the people of Lancaster County, there are some very common names. Martin and Weaver are common names among the Mennonites. In Lancaster County, those names are more common than Smith, Jones, and Johnson. Among the Amish, the most common names are Stoltzfus, Lapp, Beiler/Byler, Fisher, and Esh. A few years back, the Lancaster paper ran a story about a mailman who had 23 patrons named John Stoltzfus on his route.

Mennonites took their name from Menno Simmons. Amish got their name from Jacob Amman.

Transportation

Getting There: More visitors arrive by private car than by any other method. Buses also bring in many visitors, but the area is easily accessible by train and plane. Once you arrive, you can see the area by bus, train, car, balloon, and bicycle. In fact, the best method of touring is definitely the bicycle.

Planes: The airport in Lancaster is in the heart of the Amish Country. Airports in Harrisburg, Philadelphia, and Baltimore are relatively close.

Lancaster Airport, Route 501, Neffsville, about five miles north of Lancaster, 717-569-1221

US Air, 800-428-4322

Trains: Amtrak serves Lancaster and Coatesville from east and west. Trains run frequently between Philadelphia and Harrisburg. Easy connections are available from the major cities of the East Coast, especially New York, Washington, and Boston. The Amtrak station in Lancaster is at the corner of McGovern Avenue and North Queen Street. It's about a mile down Queen Street to the center of the city. For ticket information, call 717-291-5080.

From the Amtrak station in Lancaster, it's just a short walk across a bridge to a Days Inn. Cabs and buses serve the station and can take you to other accommodations. You can then use public transportation and escorted tours to get just about everywhere.

The Strasburg Railroad is a tourist line that will take you on a train ride through the fertile farmlands of Lancaster County. It runs from Strasburg to Paradise, where it turns around and comes back.

Buses, Intercity: Greyhound serves Lancaster. The station is at 22 W. Clay Street. Clay runs between Prince and Queen streets, about three-quarters of a mile north of Penn Square, and just a few blocks from the Amtrak station. For bus information, phone 717-397-4861.

Buses, Local: The Red Rose Transit Authority (RRTA) serves all sections of Lancaster County, except Quarryville in the southern end. You can ride a bus from Lancaster to any other town in Lancaster County. In addition to this service, there are tour buses that will pick you up at your hotel or motel. A major benefit of such a tour is the guide who can answer all your questions. The hub of the service is in the first block of North Queen Street in downtown Lancaster, where a waiting room is located. For information, call 717-397-4246.

In recent years, the RRTA has initiated service on buses that look just like trolleys. Running from June until October, the trolley works the Strasburg route. Riders can use it to make connections from Lancaster to Strasburg, and to such attractions as Dutch Wonderland and the Strasburg Railroad. Special All Day Passes make it economical to ride for the entire day.

Tour Buses and Vans:

Amish Country Tours, Route 340 between Bird-In-Hand and Intercourse, 717-768-7063

Amish Neighbors, Intercourse, 717-392-8687

Conestoga Tours, 825 E. Chestnut Street, Lancaster, 717-299-6666

Private Car: Many major highways run through the Amish Country. From east and west, U.S. 30 and the Pennsylvania Turnpike are the busiest roads. U.S. 222 is the major north-south route. (See Highways and Backroads chapter.)

Bicycles: See Bicycling chapter.

Taxis:

Airport Pickup and Delivery, 717-393-2222

Friendly Taxi, 717-392-2222 or 800-795-3278

Lancaster County Taxi, 717-626-8294

Yellow Cab, 717-397-8100

Car Rentals:

Agency Rent-A-Car, 1027 Dillerville Road, Lancaster, 717-397-3764

Avis Rentals, Lancaster Airport, Route 501, Neffsville, 717-397-1497 or 800-331-1212

Budget Car Rental, 1009 N. Prince Street, Lancaster, 717-392-4228 or 800-527-0700

Hertz Rentals, 625 E. Orange Street, Lancaster, 717-396-0000, and Lancaster Airport, Route 501, Neffsville, 717-569-2331. Or, call 800-654-3131.

National Car Rental, Liberty Street and Lititz Pike, Lancaster, 717-394-2158 or 800-227-7368

Snappy Car Rental, 1681 Manheim Pike, Lancaster, 717-569-4743

Ugly Duckling Rent-A-Car, 1761 Columbia Avenue, Lancaster, 717-393-3825 or 800-843-3825

Tours, Walking:

Historic Lancaster Walking Tour, 100 S. Queen Street, 717-392-1776

Tours, Hot-Air Balloon:

Adventures Aloft, 717-733-3777

Great Adventure Balloon Club, 717-397-3623

Lancaster Hot Air Balloons, 717-560-1937

Windwalker Entertainment, 717-872-0761

Tours, Bicycle:

New Horizons, 717-285-7607

Strasburg Bike Rentals, Route 741 and Bishop Road (near RR Museum), Strasburg, 717-687-8222

Around the County

The Amish Country has many small towns, some medium-sized ones, and several cities. If you look at a map, you'll see many places that are so tiny that you can pass through them and not even realize you were there. Here's a rundown of what you'll find when you visit the bigger towns.

Lancaster. As the county seat and the biggest city in Lancaster County, Lancaster is the hub of economic and cultural activity in the Amish Country. Superficially, Lancaster looks like many other medium-sized cities. A closer look, however, reveals some interesting differences. The biggest city in the Amish Country, it's home to about 55,000 people. Back in the 1780s, Lancaster was the biggest inland city in the U.S. Today, it has a diverse economy and an eclectic population.

Lancaster is a place where traditions are an important part of daily life. In the center of town is **Central Market,** the oldest continuously operating, publicly owned market in the country. Beside it is the **Heritage Center,** a museum featuring many items from the area's past. A block away is the **Fulton Opera House.** Built in 1852, it's still a vibrant theater, hosting many plays and concerts every year.

Lancaster isn't a place that lives solely in the past, though. Manufacturing, health care, and service industries flourish. Armstrong World Industries is the biggest employer. Franklin and Marshall College, a prestigious liberal arts institution, is in the western end of town. The downtown area is home to businesses, government, restaurants, and galleries.

Lancaster is the transportation hub of the Amish Country. Most major highways go through the city. All local bus routes begin there, and Amtrak and Greyhound stop there. Lancaster Airport is just north of the city.

Lancaster is also the communications hub of the area. The only daily newspapers and the only Sunday paper come out of Lancaster. WGAL-TV, Channel 8, is the only small-town VHF station in a large area.

On the western edge of the city is **Wheatland,** the home of James Buchanan, Pennsylvania's only president. Adjacent to Wheatland is the Lancaster County Historical Society.

Architecturally, Lancaster, like Philadelphia and Baltimore, is a city of rowhouses. It's also a city of beautiful old homes, some of which even have stained-glass windows. For a look at some of Lancaster's beautiful older homes, walk north on Duke Street or east on Orange Street.

The only good way to get a feel for Lancaster is to park the car and walk around. In area, it's actually a rather small city, so you don't have to be an endurance athlete to see many of the sights.

The central shopping district begins at Penn Square, at the intersection of King and Queen streets. It extends several blocks in every direction. The 300 block of North Queen Street is Lancaster's offbeat shopping area, with unusual offerings of clothing, glassworks, books, and music. It's not terribly unusual, however. It does have automotive stores and some traditional restaurants. Within a half mile of Penn Square, you'll find a wide variety of eating opportunities in all price ranges. For details, see Food, Drink, and Restaurants.

For information on downtown activities, visit the Downtown Investment District offices at 45 N. Market Street, or the Downtown Visitors Center at 100 S. Queen Street.

Adamstown, northeast section, at the intersection of PA 272, PA 897, U.S. 222, and the Pennsylvania Turnpike. The single word that best describes Adamstown is "antiques." (See Galleries, Crafts, and Antiques chapter.) On Sundays from March

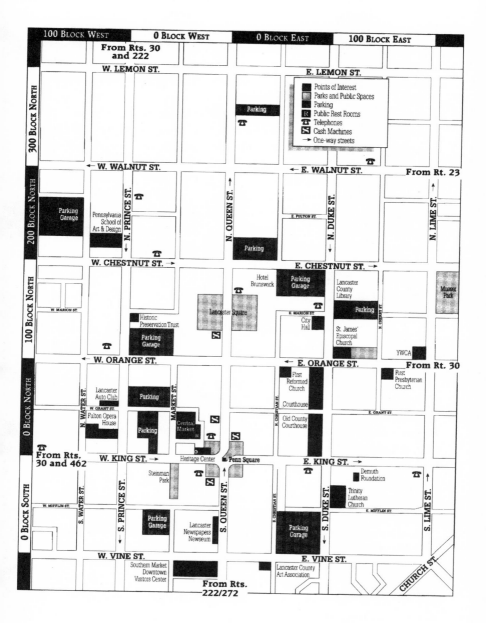

Downtown Lancaster

to November, antique buyers and sellers converge on Adamstown. Adamstown is also famous for the **Bavarian Summer Festival.** Commonly known as Gemütlichkeit (guh-MOOT-luh-kite), it's essentially a German-style beer-drinking festival.

Most of the time, Adamstown is pretty quiet. The major industry is Bollman Hats, makers of all kinds of headwear.

Akron, northeast section, on PA 272, just south of Ephrata. Akron is a quiet little town that's a major center of activities for the Mennonite Church. **The SelfHelp Crafts Warehouse** at 704 Main Street has craft items from many parts of the world. The Mennonite Church sells them and uses the proceeds to help Third World peoples help themselves. Akron is also the home of **Martin's Pretzels** at 1229 Diamond Road. Like most local pretzels, these have a cult following.

Bainbridge, western section, on PA 441 along the Susquehanna River. The main attraction in Bainbridge is the **Nissley Winery,** on Maytown Road. They offer wine tastings and special events.

A few miles north of Bainbridge on 441 is a place called **Three Mile Island.** Back in 1979, TMI became internationally famous when the nuclear power plant there threatened to melt down. At the TMI Visitor's Center are displays that explain exactly what happened.

Bird-In-Hand, central section, east of Lancaster on PA 340. Bird-In-Hand is right in the middle of Amish farm country. "Downtown" Bird-In-Hand is full of places to buy food, quilts, and crafts. **The Bird-In-Hand Farmer's Market** offers fresh produce, prepared foods, and hot meals. Nearby you can find restaurants, buggy rides, a flea market, bakeries, a general store, and much more.

Kauffman's Market is an excellent place to stock up on apples and peaches. Kauffman's Orchards are among the biggest in Lancaster County and their market is one of their major outlets. They have dozens of varieties of apples and peaches, and a full line of products made from them, such as butters, jams, and apple cider.

The Bird-In-Hand Bakery on Gibbons Road is off the beaten track but enough people find it to keep it busy. To get there, turn north from 340 onto Beechdale Road, which is just east of the railroad overpass, then go right onto Gibbons Road. The bakery is just down the road from the one-room schoolhouse.

Also off the main road is **Miller's Natural Foods,** a health food store on an Amish farm. To get there, turn north onto North Ronks Road, just east of the Farmer's Market. Then go right onto Church and left onto Monterey. Miller's is about a quarter of a mile down the road.

At the intersection of Stumptown Road and Newport Road (PA 772) is the **Mascot Roller Mill.** To get there from 340, go north on Beechdale Road to Stumptown Road. Turn right on Stumptown. The mill is at the second stop sign. This is an old-fashioned mill where they used to grind grain into flour. The mill still functions, but it stopped being profitable when area farmers stopped growing wheat and corn for flour. Now, they devote almost all of their land to growing feed crops. They could get only one crop of corn or wheat every year, but they can get as many as four or five cuttings of alfalfa.

The mill is open from May to November and there's no admission charge. When you go in, a guide will turn a wheel that allows water to rush in and power the machinery. In a few minutes, grain will become flour. Beside the mill is a meadow that's a wildlife refuge. And, the house next door has been kept just as it was when the lady who lived there left it.

Bird-In-Hand is also a good place to start a bike ride. The area is as flat as any in Lancaster County. Wherever you go, you'll be in Amish farmlands. You can easily spend a full day or two in Bird-In-Hand.

Blue Ball, eastern section, just east of New Holland at intersection of PA 23 and U.S. 322. Most of the year, Blue Ball is a busy little agricultural center. Farms surround the town and the **Shady Maple Market** on Route 23 draws shoppers from miles around. Once a year, Blue Ball livens up. The Saturday before Labor Day is Blue Ball Day. The whole town has a festival/picnic/yard sale/pancake breakfast. They block off most of the streets and have a good time.

Bowmansville, northeast section, on PA 625. Bowmansville is so small and so quiet that many Lancaster County residents would have trouble locating it on a map. Bowmansville is home to a park and a general store. Lancaster County's only youth hostel is in Bowmansville. If you enjoy meeting people and you're looking for reasonable rates, call the AYH at 717-445-4831.

Christiana, eastern section, on PA 372. Nothing much happens in Christiana, and the residents like it that way. Christiana is a beautiful small town with many large, gorgeous old homes. Life in Christiana still seems to move at a comfortable pace.

Columbia, western section, on U.S. 30, PA 462, PA 441, and Susquehanna River. This is Lancaster County's biggest river town. It's primarily a working town. At 524 Poplar Street is the **National Watch and Clock Museum,** which features a history of time and timepieces. Just north of town on Route 441 is **Chickies Rock.** It's a natural area that affords an excellent view of the Susquehanna River. For a good view of the river, drive south on 441.

Denver, northern section, on PA 272. Actually, downtown Denver is west of 272. It's a small, rural borough with several small factories, and a feed mill right in the center of town. Out on 272 is **Zinn's Diner,** a busy restaurant that features Pennsylvania Dutch cooking and baking. It also has a park, a playground, and miniature golf.

Elizabethtown, western section, on PA 230, PA 283, and PA 743. Elizabethtown is the home of Elizabethtown College, a small liberal arts institution. The E-Town Fair in late August is the earliest of Lancaster County's many agricultural fairs.

Ephrata (EF-ruh-tuh), northern section, on U.S. 322, U.S. 222, and PA 272. Ephrata has several noteworthy attractions. On Fridays throughout the year, the **Green Dragon Market** (see Farmer's Markets and Roadside Stands chapter) draws thousands of shoppers. They can buy almost anything that anyone can imagine, from food to clothes to quilts. Sometimes, there's a hay auction. Farmers bid against each other for truckloads of hay that they'll feed to their animals. Mostly, people buy food

A barn raising is a fitting symbol of how the Amish take care of each other in times of need. If a barn has burned down or a newlywed couple are just starting out, the local Amish community joins together to build a barn. (Courtesy Pennsylvania Dutch Visitors Bureau)

(Courtesy Pennsylvania Dutch Visitors Bureau)

and eat it immediately. In summer, you can buy produce that was still in the field, or on the tree, just a few hours earlier. The Green Dragon is about two miles north of Ephrata on State Street. You can also reach it from Route 272. There's a big green dragon pointing the way.

On West Main Street (Route 322) is the **Ephrata Cloister.** The Cloister Society was an 18th-century religious communal society. The 12 restored buildings display the residents' austere lifestyle. They were famous for architecture, printing, music, and calligraphy.

On North State Street is the **Donecker's** complex. They have clothing stores for men and women, with frequent fashion shows. Nearby is **The Artworks at Donecker's.** Artists and artisans sell paintings, quilts, and crafts. There are regular trade and craft shows. **The Restaurant at Donecker's** brings French cuisine to Pennsylvania Dutch Country.

Intercourse, eastern section, at junction of PA 340 and PA 772. No trip to Lancaster County would be complete without a stop in Intercourse. This little hamlet is an interesting mix of tourist attractions and stores that supply the residents. At **Zimmerman's General Store,** you're likely to see Cadillacs parked beside buggies. At **The People's Place,** you'll find films and displays that explain the culture of "The Plain People." There are also places to buy quilts, food, furniture, candles, knives, and crafts. There's a **quilt museum.** There's an information center. And, yes, there is a post office so you can send cards from Intercourse.

All the places in Intercourse are rather close together, so it can get pretty crowded at times, especially on weekends in summer.

Lititz, northern section, on PA 501 and PA 772. This is a very pretty town, with a tree-lined main street. On the square is a restaurant where patrons can dine outside in good weather.

As you pass through Lititz, you may notice an unusual smell—chocolate. The **Wilbur Chocolate Company** is right in the center of town, at 48 N. Broad Street. At the **Candy Americana Museum,** you can see how earlier generations of Americans made candy, and you can stock up at the outlet store. At 104 N. Broad Street is the **Warwick House Restaurant,** which features an all-you-can-eat chocolate dessert bar.

Just across the railroad tracks from the candy company is **Lititz Springs Park.** On holidays and other occasions, the park hosts celebrations and craft shows. The **Lititz Outdoor Art Show** fills the downtown area, usually the last Saturday in July.

The **Sturgis Pretzels** bakery at 219 E. Main Street is supposedly the oldest pretzel bakery in the United States. Visitors can see how pretzels are made, and they can even roll their own. A variety of hard and soft pretzels is available, including pretzels in the shape of a horse and buggy.

Lititz began as a home for the Moravian Church and a **Moravian Museum** is just across Main Street from the pretzel bakery. During the Christmas season, many homes in the area display Moravian stars in their windows.

Manheim, northern section, on PA 72 and PA 772. Manheim is the kind of small town where message boards in front of firehalls tout the achievements of young athletes. North of town on Route 72 is the **Mount Hope Estate.** On weekends from July to October, it hosts the **Pennsylvania Renaissance Fair,** a recreation of medieval jousts and festivals.

Just south of town, off Route 72, is **Root's Country Market and Auction.** Open on Tuesdays, it's a big market. You can buy just about anything, from food to clothes to antiques. The **Manheim Historical Society Railroad Station** is at 210 S. Charlotte Street, just west of Route 72, along the tracks in the southern end of town. Phone 717-664-3486 for hours of operation.

In early October, the **Manheim Community Fair** takes over the streets. It offers food, rides, games, and agricultural exhibits. On the Wednesday evening of the fair, the **Manheim Mile** run goes right down Main Street.

Marietta, western section, on PA 441, PA 23, PA 743, and Susquehanna River. Marietta is a small borough with a lot of big houses. Some of them even have stained-glass windows. On Front Street, antique and art shops co-exist with neighborhood taverns. It's a nice place to watch the river roll by.

Maytown, western section on PA 743. This is a picturesque little place with a beautiful town square, a few businesses, and **Three Center Square,** a popular restaurant.

Millersville, southwestern section, on PA 999. Millersville is home to Millersville University, a state-supported institution.

Mount Gretna is actually in Lebanon County, but many Lancaster Countians visit it for summer fun. Summer theater, a lake for swimming, and summer homes attract visitors. So do trails for hiking and running. To find Mount Gretna, go north on PA 72, and west on PA 117.

Mount Joy, western section, on PA 230, PA 283, and PA 772. In recent years, some Amish families have moved west and settled around Mount Joy. It's not, however, a major Amish enclave.

Just outside of town, you'll find **Groff's Farm Restaurant,** a good place to sample authentic Pennsylvania Dutch cooking.

New Holland, eastern section, on PA 23. New Holland is a rural town that doesn't draw nearly as many tourists as some of the other towns in the area. Main Street might look like a business district anywhere, if it weren't for the presence of the Amish buggies. It's a busy town, with several heavy industries. Ford New Holland produces farm and construction equipment here. Route 23 is heavily travelled by cars, trucks, and buggies.

To the south of Route 23 is one of the more interesting sights in Lancaster County. Known by local residents as **"the goat path,"** it's the bed for a highway that was never completed. In the late seventies, the Pennsylvania Department of Transportation began work on a four-lane divided highway that would link Lancaster and New Holland. They graded the roadbed and built bridges, but the money ran out just as paving was about to begin. So, they covered the bed with dirt and forgot about it. Today, cows graze on the "highway." The fight over whether to build the highway continues. Developers want it. The Amish oppose it, for it will cut up their farms, and add miles to many of their trips.

In New Holland, the biggest social event is the **Farmer's Fair.** Held early in October, it closes Main Street and turns half of the town into a carnival. The highlight of the fair is the parade. Days in advance, people stake out spots to view it. Hundreds of marching bands, drill teams, civic groups, and commercial interests strut their stuff. Awards go to the growers of all sorts of produce, much of which reaches rather large sizes.

Paradise, eastern section, on U.S. 30. Paradise is in the heart of Amish farm country, and it's the turnaround spot for the **Strasburg Railroad.** On Route 30, you'll find a variety of shops and restaurants. One of the easiest to find covered bridges is on Belmont Road, just north of Route 30.

Pequea, southwestern section, on PA 324. Pequea is popular among local residents for its outdoor recreation opportunities. The **Pequea Creek** has long been a favorite for "tubers." Tubers ride down the river in tire tubes, usually the big ones used in truck tires. Many boaters take to the water near the confluence of the Pequea Creek and the Susquehanna River.

Quarryville, southern section, on U.S. 222, PA 472, and PA 372. The southern section is the most rural section of Lancaster County, and Quarryville is the biggest town in the area, but it's not terribly big. The biggest events in town are the **Agricultural Fair** and sporting contests at the high school. On a drive through town, you'll see farm trucks and Amish buggies. South of Quarryville, on Route 222, is the **birthplace of Robert Fulton,** the inventor of the steam engine.

Strasburg, eastern section, on PA 741 and PA 896. Trains and buggies are common sights in Strasburg. Amish farms surround the town, and the Railroad Museum of Pennsylvania attracts railfans to view rolling stock from Pennsylvania's past. In addition, the Strasburg Railroad takes visitors on a nine-mile train ride to Paradise and back. There's even a motel built from cabooses. In the center of town, an ice-cream shop is very popular with visitors and locals.

Terre Hill, northeast section, off the major highways, on PA 897. Terre Hill might be the epitome of a pleasant small town. It has a few manufacturing and processing plants, several small stores and restaurants, beautiful old homes, and a nice park. It won't take long to walk from end to end. If you want to fantasize about living in a pleasant little town, visit Terre Hill. **Terre Hill Days,** held on a Saturday late in July, is a town celebration that features yard sales, a festival, lots of food, and a five-mile run.

Highways and Backroads

The Highways

Several highways pass through Lancaster County. Some have many places of interest to visitors. Others look like highways anywhere else in the country. Here's what you'll find on the different numbered roads.

U.S. 30 east of Lancaster has more tourist attractions than any other stretch of road in Lancaster County. From its intersection with PA 41 at Gap to the beginning of the bypass around Lancaster, the road is home to restaurants, motels, an amusement park, shopping centers, and many other attractions. Recent road upgrades have improved traffic flow, but it can get quite crowded.

Still, it's not all motels and restaurants. There are some farms along Route 30, and east of Route 896, the number of commercial establishments drops off considerably. If crowds bother you, skip Route 30.

Note: Do not attempt to cross Route 30 on foot. The road is wide, traffic is fast, and several fatalities have occurred.

U.S. 322 is a fairly major highway that has avoided most of the development that has come to Route 30. On most of its route through Chester and Lancaster counties, 322 passes through heavily farmed regions where roadside stands sell produce directly to the consumer. It becomes Main Street in Ephrata. West of Route 501, it enters woodlands. West of Route 72, it returns to farmland and leads to Hershey. It's a scenic road, but not a good one for a leisurely drive.

U.S. 222 and PA 272 are the main north-south routes through Lancaster County. South of Willow Street, they're comparatively lightly travelled, and they pass mostly through farm country. North of Willow Street, they pick up more traffic and pass through Lancaster city. U.S. 222 becomes a four-lane divided highway just north of Lancaster.

PA 23, east of Lancaster, passes right through the heart of Amish farm country. It's basically a working road, and quite heavily travelled. Many industries line Route 23 and trucks use the road to reach the Pennsylvania Turnpike at Morgantown. West of Lancaster, it's a suburban and rural road, often quite heavily travelled.

PA 283 is a four-lane divided highway that runs from Lancaster to the Harrisburg area. Taking 283 to 743 at Elizabethtown is the quickest way to get to Hershey from Lancaster.

PA 340 is a major road through the Amish Country. Known as the Old Philadelphia Pike, it was the original road between Lancaster and Philadelphia. Between Lancaster and Intercourse, it's home to many places of interest to visitors. Bird-In-Hand and Intercourse are two small towns that attract many visitors. In some places, the road has a shoulder wide enough to accommodate cars and buggies simultaneously.

PA 372 runs east-west across southern Lancaster County and into Chester County. It's a rural road all the way. It passes through several small towns, and it's never really commercialized.

PA 441 runs parallel to the Susquehanna River, and passes through river towns such as Washington Boro, Columbia, Marietta, and Bainbridge. Traffic is generally fairly light. Follow 441 just north of the Lancaster County line and you'll see Three Mile Island.

PA 462 is the old Route 30. It runs through the center of Lancaster and traffic is quite heavy.

PA 501 runs north from Lancaster. It's heavily travelled and the main town on the road is Lititz.

PA 625 is a country road that sometimes seems to carry more bicycles than cars. It runs northeast to Reading. The only town on 625 is Bowmansville, a quiet place that's home to Lancaster County's only youth hostel.

PA 741 begins at Gap and heads west. Until it reaches Strasburg, it's wide open with fast-moving traffic. It passes one Amish farm after another. With a steep ridge to the south, 741 is one of the prettiest stretches of highway anywhere. At the Strasburg Railroad, it becomes quite congested. Strasburg is one of the visitors' favorite towns, and they sometimes arrive in greater numbers than 741 and 896 can handle.

PA 772 will take you on a meandering tour of Lancaster County. For much of its length, it's known as Newport Road. Once, Newport Road ran from Delaware to Erie. In the eastern part of the county, 772 passes through Amish farmlands and small towns such as Intercourse, Leola, and Brownstown. Farther west, it stays in farm country and goes through Lititz, Manheim, Mount Joy, and Marietta. You can get a very good look at Lancaster County by travelling 772 from end to end.

PA 896 has two distinct sections. The shorter one runs from Route 340 south to Strasburg. It's heavily travelled and filled with motels, restaurants, and stores. South of Strasburg, 896 becomes a farm road and traffic drops off considerably.

PA 897 winds through eastern and northern Lancaster County on its way to Lebanon. It passes through small towns such as Terre Hill and Adamstown and provides a good look at farm country.

PA 999 runs from the city of Lancaster to the Susquehanna River at Washington Boro. East of Millersville, it's quite congested. West of Millersville, traffic falls off. PA 999 has an excellent shoulder for bicyclists.

Lancaster County hosts millions of visitors every year, but only a small area is really dedicated to tourism. The highways where you'll find the greatest concentrations of attractions and accommodations are U.S. 30, PA 340, PA 741, and PA 896.

The Backroads

Away from the highways and the commercial establishments is the Lancaster County that visitors really want to see. Away from the highways, life slows down. Buggies move at a leisurely pace and crops grow slowly.

On the backroads, the only traffic jams are at covered bridges, and most vehicles seem to move rather slowly. One reason for the lack of speed is that the roads are frequently narrow and winding. They're much better for buggies and bikes than for cars, buses, and trucks.

The best way to experience the Amish Country is to head for the backroads. Explore. You're bound to spot a few things that you won't see back home. For instance, you may come to a four-way street. Between New Holland and Ephrata, there's an intersection where the street sign offers a choice between North Farmersville Road, South Farmersville Road, East Farmersville Road, and West Farmersville Road. Wherever you go, you'll see one-room schools, cornfields, craft shops, and roadside stands. You'll see Amish farmers working their fields with big horses and mules.

Leaving the major highways doesn't mean that you'll be getting away from stores and roadside stands. Many businesses are on country roads, seemingly miles from customers. But, they thrive anyway. Word-of-mouth advertising spreads the word, and loyal buyers continue to come back.

If you're physically able, it's a good idea to get out of the car and take a walk or a bike ride around the country roads. In a mile or two of walking or riding, you can experience much more than you can in a day or a week of driving around. It's the same as the difference between watching a game on television and going to the stadium.

Here are a few scenic backroads.

Scenic Road—North of, and parallel to, PA 340 near Intercourse and Bird-In-Hand
  White Oak Road, north of Quarryville
  Covered Bridge Road, south of Ephrata
  Donegal Springs Road, west of Mount Joy
  Colebrook Road, from East Petersburg to Colebrook
  Irishtown Road, near Gordonville

South View Road, near Willow Street
Beaver Dam Road, near Honey Brook in Chester County
Millbach Road, near Millbach in Lebanon County
Route 372, from Christiana to the Susquehanna River

In fact, it's difficult to make even a short list of scenic roads. The Amish Country is full of them.

Lodging

In the Amish Country, you'll find a wide variety of accommodations, from luxury resorts to economical motels. The price range is wide, even at the same facility. Some motels have four different rates for the different times of the year. A room that's $90 in July may be $50 in January. This is a rough guide to the seasons, in descending order of expense:

1. June, July, and August
2. September and October
3. April and May
4. November, December, January, February, and March

At some facilities, weekend rates are higher than weekday rates. As a general rule, the rates in the Amish Country are moderate. A 1991 survey found the average for lodging to be $66.29 per room per night.

Rates

The following codes are used in this chapter to identify an establishment's rate range:

E—Expensive; more than $95 for a double room
M—Moderate; from $65 to $94 for a double room
I—Inexpensive; less than $65 for a double room

Most of the less expensive motels offer basic accommodations without a lot of frills. They're clean, comfortable, and

71

usually run by families who know the area quite well and can answer all of your questions.

The more expensive places offer just about every creature comfort known to man. You can play golf and tennis, swim in heated pools, and eat. Remember that advance reservations are always a good idea, and a necessity in busy seasons.

Akron

Motel Akron, *I,* 116 S. Seventh Street (PA 272), 717-859-1654.

Bird-in-Hand

Along Spruce Lane Motor Lodge, *I,* on PA 340, 717-393-1991 or 800-446-4901.

Amish Country Motel, *I/M,* on PA 340, 717-768-8396 or 800-538-2535.

Bird-In-Hand Family Inn, *M,* on PA 340, 717-768-8271 or 800-537-2535.

Mill Stream Motor Lodge, *I/M,* 170 Eastbrook Road (PA 896), 717-299-0931.

Smoketown Motor Lodge, *I,* 190 Eastbrook Road (PA 896), 717-397-6944.

Village Inn of Bird-In-Hand, *E,* on PA 340, 717-293-8639. Restored 1852 inn.

Columbia

West Motel, *I,* on PA 462, 717-684-2636.

Denver

Econo Lodge, *I,* on PA 272, 717-336-4649.
Holiday Inn, *M,* on PA 272, 717-336-7541.
Howard Johnson Lodge, *M/E,* on PA 272, 717-336-7563.
Penn Amish Motel, *I,* on PA 272, 717-336-3848.
Pennsylvania Dutch Motel, *I,* on PA 272, 717-336-5559.

Elizabethtown

Conewago Valley Motor Inn, *I/M,* 1688 Hershey Road (PA 743), 717-367-4320.

Ephrata

The Guesthouse at Donecker's, *E,* 318-24 N. State Street, 717-738-9502.

Dutchmaid Motel, *I,* on PA 272 north of U.S. 322, 717-733-1720.

Smithton Country Inn, *E,* 900 W. Main Street (U.S. 322), 717-733-6094.

Hershey

Chocolatetown Motel, *M,* on PA 422 East, 717-533-2330.

Hotel Hershey, *E,* Hotel Road, near Hershey Park, 717-533-2171.

Intercourse

Best Western Intercourse Village Motor Inn, *I/M,* on PA 772, south of PA 340, 717-768-3636 or 800-528-1234.

Harvest Drive Family Motel, *I,* Clearview Road, south of PA 340, off highways, 717-768-7186 or 800-233-0176.

Traveler's Rest Motel, *I/M,* 3701 Old Philadelphia Pike (PA 340), 717-768-8731 or 800-626-2021.

Lancaster

Best Western Eden Resort Inn, *M/E,* on Eden Road at intersection of U.S. 30 and U.S. 222, 717-569-6444 or 800-528-1234. Centrally located; offers restaurants, lounges, health club.

Brunswick Hotel, *M,* Chestnut and Queen streets, 717-397-4801. Only hotel in downtown Lancaster. Popular with tour groups. Restaurants, indoor pool, exercise room, movie theaters. Within walking distance of Central Market, Fulton Opera House, and shopping.

Classic Inn, *M,* 2302 Lincoln Highway East (U.S. 30), 717-291-4576.

Continental Motor Inn, *M,* 2285 Lincoln Highway East (U.S. 30), 717-299-0421.

Country Living Motor Inn, *I/M,* 2406 Old Philadelphia Pike (PA 340), 717-295-7295.

Days Inn East, *M/E,* 34 PA 896 North, 717-390-1800 or 800-325-2525.

Days Inn Lancaster, *M/E,* 30 Keller Avenue, just west of U.S. 222, beside Amtrak station, 717-299-5700 or 800-325-2525.

Econo Lodge, *I,* 2140 Lincoln Highway East (U.S. 30), 717-397-1900 or 800-424-4777.

Econo Lodge, *I,* 2165 Lincoln Highway East (U.S. 30), 717-299-6900 or 800-424-4777.

Friendship Inn Italian Villa, *M,* 2331 Lincoln Highway East (U.S. 30), 717-397-4973.

Fulton Steamboat Inn, *M/E,* at intersection of U.S. 30 and PA 896, 717-299-9999. A motel designed to look like a steamboat.

Garden Spot Motel, *I,* 2291 Lincoln Highway East (U.S. 30), 717-394-4736.

Hampton Inn, *M,* on U.S. 30 East at Greenfield Road exit, 717-299-1200.

Hilton Garden Inn, *M/E,* 101 Granite Run Road, near intersection of PA 72 and PA 283, 717-560-0880 or 800-HILTONS. Features Business Center with personal computer, Fax machine, and other office equipment.

Holiday Inn East, *M/E,* on U.S. 30 East at Greenfield Road exit, 717-299-2551.

Holiday Inn North, *M/E,* 1492 Lititz Pike (PA 501), 717-393-0771.

Howard Johnson Lodge, *M,* 2100 Lincoln Highway East (U.S. 30), 717-397-7781.

Knights Inn Lancaster, *M,* 2151 Lincoln Highway East (U.S. 30), 717-299-8971 or 800-920-5050.

Lampeter Inn, *I,* on PA 896, just north of U.S. 30, 717-393-2550.

Lancaster Host Resort, *E,* 2300 Lincoln Highway East (U.S. 30), 717-299-5500 or 800-233-0121. Offers 27 holes of golf, 12 tennis courts, indoor and outdoor pools. Adjacent to Amish farms.

Lancaster Motel, *I/M,* 2628 Lincoln Highway East (U.S. 30), 717-687-6241.

Lincoln Motor Lodge, *I,* 2451 Lincoln Highway East (U.S. 30), 717-299-8971.

McIntosh Inn, *I/M,* 2307 Lincoln Highway East (U.S. 30), 717-299-9700 or 800-444-2775.

Motel Canadiana, *I,* 2390 Lincoln Highway East (U.S. 30), 717-397-6531.

Olde Hickory Inn & Resort, *I/M,* 2363 Oregon Pike (PA 272 North), 717-569-0477. Golf, swimming, and tennis. Very close to Landis Valley Museum.

Parkside Motel, *I,* 1310 Harrisburg Pike, 717-397-4911. Adjacent to Franklin and Marshall College athletic fields; close to Park City shopping mall.

Quality Inn, Sherwood Knoll, *M,* 500 Centerville Road, at U.S. 30, west of Lancaster, 717-898-2431 or 800-223-8963.

Ramada Inn Lancaster, *M/E,* 2250 Lincoln Highway East (U.S. 30), 717-393-5499 or 800-272-6232.

Rockvale Village Inn, *M,* on U.S. 30 East, in Rockvale Square outlet center, 717-293-9500.

1722 Motor Lodge, *I,* 1722 Old Philadelphia Pike (PA 340), 717-397-4791.

Sunset Valley Motel, *I,* 2288 New Holland Pike (PA 23 East), 717-656-2091.

Super 8 Motel, *I,* 2129 Lincoln Highway East (U.S. 30), 717-393-8888.

Travelodge, *M,* 2101 Columbia Avenue (PA 462 West), 717-397-4201.

Weathervane Motor Court, *I,* at intersection of PA 896 and U.S. 30, 717-397-3398.

Westfield Inn, *I/M,* Centerville Road at U.S. 30, west of Lancaster, 717-397-9300.

Willow Valley Resort Inn, *M/E,* 2416 Willow Street Pike (U.S. 222 South), 717-464-2711. Pools, smorgasbord, saunas, whirlpool, 9-hole golf course, playground.

Your Place Country Inn, *I/M,* 2133 Lincoln Highway East (U.S. 30), 717-393-3413.

Lebanon

Quality Inn, *M/E,* PA 72 South, close to Mount Gretna, Hershey, and Cornwall Furnace, 717-273-6771.

Leola

Zook's Motel, *I,* 103 E. Main Street (PA 23), 717-656-3313.

Lititz

501 Motel, *I,* 1355 Furnace Hills Pike (PA 501 North), 717-626-2597. Close to Speedwell Forge Lake.

General Sutter Inn, *M,* 14 E. Main Street, on the square at PA 501, 717-626-2115. Easy walking distance to Sturgis pretzel bakery, Wilbur Chocolate Factory, and Lititz Springs Park.

Manheim

Mount Hope Motel, *I,* 2845 Lebanon Road (PA 72 North), 717-665-3118.

Mount Vernon Motel, *I,* 980 Lebanon Road (PA 72 North), 717-665-9238.

Penn's Woods Motel, *I,* 2931 Lebanon Road (PA 72 North), 717-665-2755.

Marietta

Blue Note Motor Inn, *I,* PA 441, three miles north of U.S. 30, 717-426-1991.

Morgantown

Wilson World Hotel, *M,* at Exit 22 of PA Turnpike, directly beside Manufacturers Outlet Mall, 215-286-3000 or 800-248-2276.

Mount Joy

Cameron Estate Inn, *M/E,* Donegal Springs Road, 717-653-1773. Far off beaten paths. Restored 1805 estate with fireplaces and acres of woodlands.

New Holland

Country Squire Motor Inn, *I,* 504 E. Main Street (PA 23), 717-354-4166.

Paradise

Best Western Revere Motor Inn, *I/M,* 3063 Lincoln Highway East (U.S. 30), 717-687-7683 or 800-528-1234.

Ronks

Cherry Lane Motor Inn, *I,* 84 N. Ronks Road, 717-687-7646.

Countryside Motel, *I,* 134 Hartman Bridge Road (PA 896), 717-687-8931.

Olde Amish Inn, *I,* 33 Eastbrook Road (PA 896), 717-393-3100.

Quiet Haven Motel, *I,* 2556 Siegrist Road, 717-397-6231.

Soudersburg

Soudersburg Motel, *M,* on U.S. 30, 717-687-7607.

Strasburg

Amish Lanterns Motel, *I/M,* north on PA 896, 717-687-7839.

Carriage House Motor Inn, *I,* 144 E. Main Street, 717-687-7651.

Dutch Treat Motel, *I,* 265 Herr Road, off PA 896, 717-687-7998.

Hershey Farm Motor Inn, *M,* on PA 896 north of town, 717-687-8635.

Historic Strasburg Inn, *E,* on PA 896 north of town, 717-687-7691 or 800-872-0201.

Red Caboose Motel, *M,* PA 791 east of Strasburg Railroad, 717-687-5000. Motel rooms are real cabooses. Strasburg Railroad trains pass beside motel. Buggy rides on premises. All railroad attractions nearby.

Timberline Lodges, *M,* 44 Summit Hill Drive, 717-687-7472. Far off highways.

Youth Hostel

American Youth Hostel, *I,* PA 625, Bowmansville, 717-445-4831. A favorite stopping place for bicyclists passing through or touring the area, the hostel offers inexpensive accommodations and an opportunity to meet other travellers. There are some restrictions on time and behavior, and guests are expected to perform housekeeping chores.

Farm Vacations

Imagine being awakened at the crack of dawn by the crowing

of a rooster. Then you get up and work on the farm all day. That's an option that's available to you through the **Pennsylvania Farm Vacation Association.** Approximately 40 farms around the state are involved in this program, and about 40 percent of them are in the Amish Country. The association regularly inspects the farms to make sure that they meet certain standards. Rates vary according to meal plans and types of accommodations.

If you do stay on a farm, you don't have to work, but a day in the fields will greatly increase your understanding of the hard work involved in farming. Before you head off to the farm, here are some tips.

First, make your reservations well in advance. Accommodations are limited. Remember that the farm family's primary occupation is running the farm. Don't expect the same kind of luxurious facilities as you'll find in a fancy hotel.

Guests often share bathrooms. Don't be surprised if the farm family goes to bed early. Above all, expect to see a way of life that's considerably different from yours.

Here is a list of farm vacation sites in the Amish Country:

Cedar Hill Farm, 305 Longenecker Road, Mount Joy, PA 17552, 717-653-4655

Cherry Crest Dairy Farm, 150 Cherry Hill Road, Ronks, PA 17572, 717-687-6844

Green Acres Farm, 1382 Pinkerton Road, Mount Joy, PA 17552, 717-653-4028

Landis Farm, 2048 Gochlan Road, Manheim, PA 17545, 717-898-7028

Olde Fogie Farm, RD 1, Box 166, Marietta, PA 17547, 717-426-3992

Penn's Valley Farm, RD 7, Box 385, Manheim, PA, 717-898-7386

Pleasant Grove Farm, 368 Pilottown Road, Peach Bottom, PA 17563, 717-548-3100

Rayba Acres Farm, 183 Black Horse Road, Paradise, PA 17562, 717-687-6729

Rocky Acre Farm, 1020 Pinkerton Road, Mount Joy, PA 17552, 717-653-4449

Spahr's Century Farm, 192 Green Acre Road, Lititz, PA 17543, 717-627-2185

Stone Haus Farm, 360 Esbenshade Road, Manheim, PA 17545, 717-653-5819

Verdant View Farm, 429 Strasburg Road, Paradise, PA 17562, 717-687-7353

Vogt Farm, 1225 Colebrook Road, Marietta, PA, 717-653-4810

For a current brochure on farm vacations, write to:
Farm Vacations
PA Department of Agriculture, Domestic Trade Division
2301 N. Cameron Street, Harrisburg, PA 17110-9408

Bed and Breakfasts

In the past decade, bed and breakfast inns have become quite popular, and quite numerous, in the Amish Country. A bed and breakfast provides a personal touch that a hotel or motel can't match. Normally, the inn is the owners' home. The owners actually prepare meals and meet all of their guests.

Bed and breakfast inns aren't necessarily less expensive than other accommodations. With their smaller number of rooms and personalized services, they can't match the prices of large budget motels, but they do offer many important amenities. Rates range from about $40 to $115.

If you want to stay in a bed and breakfast, it's imperative to make advance reservations. Many b&b's have just a few rooms. In addition, many are off the major roads and you'll need to get accurate directions to locate them. Since they're run by families, many b&b's are unable to accept credit cards. By calling well in advance, you can make all arrangements before you arrive.

An asterisk (*) indicates a bed and breakfast that's well off the major roads.

Adamstown Inn, 62 W. Main Street, Adamstown, 19501, 215-

484-0800 or 800-594-4808.

Alden House B & B, 62 E. Main Street, Lititz, 17543, 717-627-3363.

Apple Bin Inn, 2835 Willow Street Pike, Willow Street, 17584, 717-464-5881.

Apple Blossom Inn, 117 E. Main Street, Terre Hill, 215-445-9466.

Australian Walkabout Inn, 837 Village Road, Lampeter, 17537, 717-464-0707.

Bed & Breakfast—The Manor, 830 Village Road, Lampeter, 17537, 717-464-9564.

Ben-Mar Tourist Home, 5721 Old Philadelphia Pike, Gap, 17527, 717-768-3309.

Benner's Country Home, 206 N. Ronks Road, Ronks, 17572, 717-299-2615.

Boxwood Inn, Diamond Road and Tobacco Road, Akron, 800-238-3466 (nonsmoking).

*Brownstone Corner B & B, 590 Galen Road, Reinholds, 17569, 717-484-4460.

Carriage Corner B & B, 3705 E. Newport Road, Intercourse, 717-768-3059 or 800-209-3059.

Carriage House Manor, 143 W. Main Street, Mountville, 17554, 717-285-5497.

Carter Run Inn, 511 E. Main Street, Lititz, 17543, 717-626-8807.

*Cedar Hill Farm, 305 Longenecker Road, Mount Joy, 17552, 717-653-4655.

Cherry Crest Farm, 150 Cherry Hill Road, Ronks, 17572, 717-687-6844.

*Chrisken Inn, 4035 Garfield Road, Mount Joy, 17554, 717-653-2717.

Churchtown Inn B & B, PA 23, Churchtown, 17555, 215-445-7794.

*Clearview Farm, 355 Clearview Road, Ephrata, 17522, 717-733-6333.

The Columbian, 360 Chestnut Street, Columbia, 17512, 800-422-5869.

Cook's Guest House, 22 W. Penn Grant Road, Willow Street,

*Country Cottage B & B, 163 Magnolia Drive, Holtwood, 17532, 717-284-2559.

*Country Farm House, 507 Beechdale Road, Bird-In-Hand, 17505, 656-4625.

*Country Pines Farm & Cottage, 1101 Auction Road, Manheim, 17545, 717-665-5478.

*Creekside Inn B & B, 44 Leacock Road, Paradise, 17562, 717-687-0333.

*The Decoy B & B, 958 Eisenberger Road, Strasburg, 17579, 717-687-8585.

Farmer's Valley, RD 4, Box 537, E. Farmersville Road, Ephrata, 17522, 717-354-0714.

*Frogtown Acres B & B, 44 Frogtown Road, Paradise, 17562, 717-768-7684.

*Green Acres Farm, 1382 Pinkerton Road, Mount Joy, 17554, 717-653-4028.

Greystone Manor, PA 340, Box 270, Bird-In-Hand, 17505, 717-393-4233.

Hillside Farm, 607 Eby Chiques Road, Mount Joy, 717-653-6697 (nonsmoking).

Hilltop Tourist Home, 3422 W. Newport Road, Ronks, 717-768-3468.

*Hollinger Farm B & B, 2336 Hollinger Road, Lancaster, 17602, 717-464-3050.

King's Cottage B & B, 1049 E. King Street, Lancaster, 17602, 800-747-8717 (*se habla español*).

Limestone Inn, 33 E. Main Street, Strasburg, 17579, 717-687-8392.

Lincoln Haus Inn, 1687 Lincoln Highway East, Lancaster, 17602, 717-392-9412 (nonsmoking).

Manheim Manor, 140 S. Charlotte Street, Manheim, 717-664-4168 or 800-MANOR11.

*Maple Lane Farm, 505 Paradise Lane, Paradise, 17562, 717-687-7479.

Meadowview Guest House, 2169 New Holland Pike, Lancaster, 17601, 717-299-4017.

Neffdale Farm, Strasburg Road, Paradise, 17562, 717-687-7837.

Nissly's Lancaster City Inn, 624 W. Chestnut Street, Lancaster, 17603, 717-392-2311.

O'Flaherty's Dingeldein House, 1105 E. King Street, Lancaster, 17602, 717-293-1723.

Old Road Guest House, 2501 Old Philadelphia Pike, Smoketown, 17576, 717-393-8182.

Oregon B & B, 1500 Oregon Road, Leola, 17540, 717-656-6201.

*The Osceola Mill House, 313 Osceola Mill Road, Gordonville, 17529.

Patchwork Inn, 2319 Old Philadelphia Pike, Lancaster, 17602, 717-293-9078.

Rocky Acre Farm, 1020 Pinkerton Road, Mount Joy, 17552, 717-653-4449.

Runnymede Farm, 1020 Robert Fulton Highway, Quarryville, 17566, 717-786-3625.

*Stauffer's Country Home, 954 Hossler Road, Manheim, 17545, 717-665-7327.

Strasburg Village Inn, 1 W. Main Street, Strasburg, 17579, 800-541-1055.

Verdant View Farm, 429 Strasburg Road, Paradise, 17562, 717-687-7353.

*Walnut Hill Farm B & B, 801 Walnut Hill Road, Millersville, 17551, 717-872-2283.

Wildflowers, 354 Rudy Dam Road, Lititz, 17543, 717-626-2156.

*Winding Glen Farm, 107 Noble Road, Christiana, 17509, 215-593-5535.

Witmer's Tavern—Historic 1715 Inn, 2014 Old Philadelphia Pike, Lancaster, 17602, 717-299-5305. Lancaster's only pre-Revolutionary inn still housing travellers.

Campgrounds

Camping isn't what it used to be. Most of the roughing it is just a memory. Today's campground offers just about all the conveniences and comforts of home. If you don't own an RV, you can rent a camper or a cabin at many campgrounds. You'll also find a wide range of activities, from swimming to hiking to horseback riding to square dancing.

Lancaster County has thousands of campsites, but finding an open one can be difficult, so it's important to call ahead. The dates of operation vary. Most campgrounds open around April 1, but some are open all year.

Beacon Camping Lodge, Intercourse, 717-768-8775. April 1—November 1.

Cocalico Creek Campground, Denver, 215-267-2014. April 8—October 15.

Country Acres Family Campground, Gordonville, 717-687-8014.

Country Haven Campground, New Holland, 717-354-7926. Open all year.

Dutch Cousin Campsite, Denver, 215-267-6911. Open all year.

Flory's Camping & Cottages, Ronks, 717-687-6670. Open all year.

Hershey-Conewago KOA Kampground, Elizabethtown, 717-367-1179. April 1—October 24.

Hickory Run Campground, Denver, 215-267-5564. April 1—November 1.

Lake In Woods Campground, Narvon, 215-445-5525. April 1—November 1.

Lancaster-Reading KOA Kampground, Denver, 215-267-2112. April 1—November 1.

Mill Bridge Village and Campresort, Strasburg, 717-687-8181. March 15—November 30.

Muddy Run Recreation Park, Holtwood, 717-484-4587. April 1—November 24.

Oak Creek Camping & Trailer Reservation, Bowmansville, 215-445-6161. March 15—November 15.

Olde Forge Recreation Park, Holtwood, 717-284-2591. April 15—November 15.

Old Mill Stream Camping Manor, Lancaster, 717-299-2314. Open all year.

Outdoor World, 2111 Millersville Road, Lancaster, 717-872-4651. Open all year.

Pequea Creek Campground, Pequea, 717-284-4587. April 15—October 15. Open all year for primitive camping.

Pinch Pond Campground, Manheim, 717-665-7640. April 15—October 31.

Promised Land Christian Camp, Conestoga, 717-872-5403. Memorial Day—Labor Day.

Ridge Run Campground, Elizabethtown, 717-367-3454. April 1—November 1.

Roamers Retreat Campground, Kinzers, 717-442-4287. April 1—November 1.

Rustic Meadows Camping & Golf Resort, Elizabethtown, 717-367-7718. Open all year.

Shady Grove Campground, PA 897, Adamstown, 215-484-4225. April 1—November 1.

Sill's Family Campground, Adamstown, 215-484-4806. April 1—October 30.

Spring Gulch Resort Campground, New Holland, 717-354-3100. April 1—November 1.

Starlite Camping Resort, Stevens, 717-734-9655. April 1—November 1.

Sun Valley Campground, Bowmansville, 215-445-6262. April 1—October 24.

Tucquan Park Family Campground, 917 River Road, Holtwood, 717-284-2156. April 1—November 1.

White Oak Campground, Quarryville, 717-687-6207. Open all year.

Woodland Acres Family Campground, Quarryville, 717-786-3458. April 1—October 31.

Yogi Bear's Jellystone Park Camp Resort, 340 Blackburn Road, Quarryville, 717-786-3458. April 1—October 31.

Food, Drink, and Restaurants

In the Amish Country, you'll find many foods that are local favorites, but which may be practically unknown, or at least much less popular, elsewhere. Here are descriptions of some of the local favorites.

Potato Chips

If you stop in a local supermarket and take a stroll down the snack aisle, you'll see a display that you won't see in most other parts of the country. The shelves are full of potato chips, sometimes as many as 17 different brands, most of them locally made. Lancaster and surrounding counties make up the unofficial Potato Chip Capital of the world.

Nobody seems to know why the region is home to so many chip makers. Potatoes aren't native to the area, but they have won a loyal following. For many local residents, chips are one of life's great sensual pleasures. They're inexpensive, but a real threat to the waistline.

Chip companies come in all sizes. Herr's is one of the nation's biggest producers, using millions of pounds of potatoes every year in a highly automated plant. Zerbe's is tiny and does the work by hand, but each brand has a distinctive taste, and followers who wouldn't buy any other brand, except when they can't find their favorites. The competition for the chip buyer's dollar is fierce, and companies frequently discount their products. To say which brand is tastiest is impossible. Everyone has a favorite.

If you'd like to see how chips are made, the best place to visit is:

Herr's Chips, Route 272, Nottingham, 800-523-5030. Plant tours and free samples available.

Other delicious local brands are: Martin's, Utz's, Groff's, Moyer's, Stehman's, Zerbe's, Good's, Middleswarth's, Snyder's, and Bickel's.

Pretzels

Just as popular as chips are pretzels, which are also a major regional industry. The city of Reading, in Berks County, calls itself "Pretzel City." Anderson Pretzel Bakery, in Lancaster, is the world's largest. Sturgis Pretzel Bakery, in Lititz, was supposedly the world's first.

In the Amish Country, you'll find a great variety of pretzels. They come in various sizes and shapes, hard and soft. There's almost no limit to the things that people can do with dough and salt. Philadelphia is famous for its "saw" (soft) pretzels, but they don't stand up well in comparison to the Lancaster County cousins.

Among Lancaster County natives, the favorite pretzels are Hammond's. The company operates in a small bakery tucked into a residential neighborhood, and the green and orange cans are familiar sights in local homes.

Mumma's is another small company with a fine collection of hard and soft pretzels. Auntie Anne's is a rapidly growing chain of soft-pretzel stands that has won a strong following.

A visit to any of the pretzel bakeries may surprise you. With the exception of Anderson's, they maintain the Lancaster County tradition of small, utilitarian operations, and some still roll pretzels by hand. To see pretzels made, these are the best places to visit.

Anderson Pretzels, 2060 Old Philadelphia Pike, Lancaster, 717-299-2321

Hammond's Pretzels, 716 S. West End Avenue, Lancaster, 717-392-7532

Mumma's Pretzels, 614 Fourth Street, Lancaster, 717-394-1569. Also visit their stand at Central Market.

Sturgis Pretzels, 219 E. Main Street, Lititz, 717-626-4354. Here, you can twist your own pretzels.

Other Favorite Local Foods

Shoo-Fly Pie: You may have heard of this Pennsylvania Dutch favorite. Despite its name, it doesn't actually contain flies. The name comes from early settlers who had to shoo the flies away from the sweet and sticky pies. The main ingredient is molasses, with flour, sugar, and shortening added. It doesn't qualify as a nutritional powerhouse, but it is tasty. You can find shoo-fly pies in stores, at markets, and at roadside stands.

Red Beet Eggs: If you're in a market, and you see eggs that aren't an egg's normal color, they're probably red beet eggs. They're produced by soaking hard-boiled eggs in the juice of pickled red beets. In Lancaster County, these are a favorite. They're available in many convenience stores as a snack item.

A note of caution: Eggs are a breeding ground for salmonella, a major cause of food poisoning. If you buy any eggs, or egg products, keep them refrigerated.

Apple Fritters: These are the apple's equivalent of french fries. They're slices of apple breaded and deep fried in oil. They're available in many markets, and at fairs.

Funnel Cakes: These are batter that's funneled into hot fat to create rings around rings. Watching somebody make them is just about as interesting as eating them. You'll find funnel cakes at any self-respecting social/eating event in Lancaster County.

Fasnachts: These yeast doughnuts are probably the only food that has a day named for them. In Lancaster County, Shrove Tuesday, the day before Ash Wednesday, is Fasnacht Day. Tradition demands that local residents eat fasnachts on this day. Fasnachts are actually deep-fried doughnuts. Usually, they're rectangular, with a slit cut in the center. Bakeries do a brisk business on Fasnacht Day.

Sauerkraut: This fermented cabbage dish has long been a Lancaster County staple. In fact, a part of the city of Lancaster is known as Cabbage Hill, because the German settlers grew cabbages in their gardens. Pennsylvania Dutch tradition calls for sauerkraut, usually with pork and mashed potatoes, on New Year's Day. The Leola Fire Company has a big sauerkraut dinner on New Year's Day, and hot dogs at football games usually have sauerkraut as an optional topping.

Root Beer: At many Amish roadside stands, and at places such as the Green Dragon Market, homemade root beer is available. In some places, you'll find birch beer beside the root beer. Usually, you can buy it by the cup or in gallon jugs. On a hot summer day, it's a great thirst quencher.

Horseradish: A favorite local condiment is horseradish sauce. It's hot and pungent and guaranteed to liven up anything that you eat. The best place to buy fresh horseradish is at Long's in Central Market in Lancaster. The family has been grinding it on the spot for decades, and a fan blows the fragrance toward passing shoppers.

What's Growing Out There

Since the Amish Country is an agricultural area, visitors often wonder just what is growing in all those verdant fields. Farmers plant four major crops, and dozens of minor ones. As tastes, health concerns, and farm economics change, however, so do the crops that farmers plant.

The four biggest crops are corn, soybeans, alfalfa, and tobacco. The corn, soybeans, and alfalfa are generally used to feed animals.

Corn is the easiest crop to identify because it's the tallest. Stalks generally grow to heights of six to eight feet in large fields. **Soybeans** grow much closer to the ground. They're green plants with hairy little pods. In addition to animal feed, they end up as margarine, as tofu (the bean curd found in Chinese restaurants), and as ingredients in hundreds of processed food products.

Alfalfa is a grass that farmers feed to livestock. It generally grows about three to four feet tall. If you see a farmer making hay, he's probably cutting alfalfa. In a good year, farmers can get

Corn awaiting harvest.

four or five cuttings of alfalfa. Like lawn grasses, it continues to grow until cold weather makes it dormant.

The **tobacco** plant has many large leaves growing from a center stalk on plants from three to four feet high. Most of the tobacco grown in Lancaster County goes into cigars. Tobacco was once a much more important crop, but the health hazards associated with it have caused many farmers to stop growing it.

In addition to those four crops, you can find somebody growing just about everything that will grow at 40° North latitude. By mid-July, **tomatoes** are everywhere. The most popular local tomatoes come from Washington Boro, a small town along the Susquehanna River just south of Columbia. The arrival of the first Washington Boro tomatoes is always cause for celebration and a newspaper story. There's no real secret to choosing good tomatoes. They will ripen after they're picked, so it's fine to pick them before they're completely red.

Sweet corn is another major local favorite. Just about everybody loves corn on the cob. In July and August, market stands and roadside wagons are piled high with fresh corn. Churches, clubs, and fire companies sponsor corn roasts as fund raisers.

Commercially grown corn comes in two colors—white and yellow. Silver Queen is the preferred white variety, and it dominates the market. Sometimes, it's actually difficult to find yellow sweet corn. In recent years, hybrids with names such as Bread and Butter have combined white and yellow kernels on the same ear and become quite popular.

There are some tips for buying and enjoying corn. First, bigger is usually better. The tastiest corn has ears that are big and kernels that are completely filled out. When kernels have an indentation on top, they're old and losing moisture. If you can find it, buy corn directly from the farm. That way, you can be sure that it's fresh, and the price will usually be lower. Generally, you can get fresh corn from late June until late October, with a peak in July and August.

In Lancaster County, corn finds its way into a variety of dishes—muffins, fritters, puddings, and pies. Chicken corn soup is a local favorite that shows up at many community events.

Beans are a common complement for corn. In societies around the world, people have combined grains and legumes for thousands of years. The Orient has rice and soybeans. North America has corn and beans. In the Amish Country, you'll find a variety of beans. Wherever you find fresh corn, you'll also find beans.

Peas are beans' close cousin in the legume family. Sugar peas are something of a delicacy, and one of the earliest crops to reach market, usually in May. Hull peas, or green peas, come a little later, and the supply lasts longer.

Celery is a Lancaster County favorite that is available all year, but only a few growers produce it. Hodecker's Celery Farm, on Route 72 in East Petersburg, is the biggest local seller. When you drive past, you can actually smell the celery in the fields. Hodecker's has a stand at Central Market.

Broccoli and **cauliflower** hit market twice a year—in late spring and in fall. These crops grow well in cool weather, and tend to wilt in summer's heat. A common misconception about cauliflower is that it's naturally white. Actually, growers tie the leaves over the heads to prevent them from developing color. It tastes just as good if it's not perfectly white, however.

Cabbage is a Pennsylvania Dutch staple. Growers produce large quantities of green cabbage, and smaller quantities of red or purple cabbage.

Asparagus is a spring vegetable, and just about every farm has an asparagus patch. Supplies are best in May, and almost completely gone by June.

Dozens of different varieties of **squash** make their way to market. Zucchini types come first, and glut the market in the heat of summer. No plants grow and produce more prolifically than squash plants. In late summer and autumn, butternut and other hard squashes are abundant. Pumpkins are close relatives of squashes.

You might be surprised to learn that Pennsylvania's biggest cash crop is **mushrooms.** The mushroom industry is concentrated around Kennett Square in Chester County. One reason why mushrooms are such a big crop is that they grow indoors, without light, so they can grow all year.

Fruits

The Amish Country is not a major fruit-producing region, but you can still find a nice variety. Apples, peaches, cantaloupes, cherries, strawberries, and raspberries are the most common locally grown fruits.

The first **apples** reach market around the middle of July. Thanks to modern storage methods, they're available all year. October is the best month, and many apple products, and cider, are plentiful. Kauffman's Market on Route 340 in Bird-In-Hand and at Central Market in Lancaster has an excellent selection of apples and apple products.

Apple festivals are common. A big one takes place at Landis Valley Museum in early October. The Ephrata Cloister museum has an Apple Dumpling Festival in early October, and the agricultural fairs all pay homage to apples.

Here's an interesting food fact: Despite the popularity of the phrase "as American as apple pie," apples are actually an exotic fruit. They came here with European immigrants.

The first **peaches** ripen around the middle of July. Various varieties are available until the end of September. Kauffman's is also big on peaches, but nobody was big on peaches in 1994. The brutal winter killed all the buds, and the trees produced almost no fruit.

Cherries begin in late May and have too brief a stay. By the beginning of July, they're just a sweet memory. At Cherry Hill Orchards on Long Lane in New Danville (717-872-9311), you can pick your own cherries at a price much lower than you'd pay otherwise.

Strawberries also come in late May. Strawberry festivals are common in June. If you'd like to pick your own strawberries (not an easy task), check the classified section of the local papers under "Produce." Many farms allow people to come and pick their own.

Cantaloupes become more of a cash crop every year. For a couple of weeks in August, farmers practically beg people to take them. Melons that might sell for a dollar in a store sell for a quarter at a roadside stand. Keep a spoon with you when you travel through the area.

Raspberries come in red and black varieties, and you can either buy them or get them free. They grow wild, usually along the edge of a wooded area. If you're hiking or biking, you're bound to spot some. It's fairly common to see people out gathering their own berries.

You will also find **blackberries** and **mulberries** growing almost everywhere, but you won't find them in stores because they're too fragile to transport.

Many other fruits grow locally in small quantities, such as **watermelons, pears,** and **plums**. If you want to see Pennsylvania's biggest fruit-growing region, head out to Adams County. The area around Biglerville, just a few miles north of Gettysburg, is home to many large orchards. It's especially beautiful in late April and early May, when all the trees are in bloom.

Nuts

There's really no nut producing industry in the Amish Country, but you can find a few **walnuts** and **chestnuts** at market stands. Walnuts come in two varieties—English and black. The English are better, and the black are more common.

Once, chestnut trees were almost everywhere. Just about every city and town in Pennsylvania has a Chestnut Street, but a blight wiped out almost all of the trees. Most of the chestnuts available now are actually a Chinese variety. Much more common than chestnut trees are **horse chestnut** trees, which Longfellow immortalized in his poem "The Village Blacksmith." Horse chestnuts are bitter and inedible, although squirrels seem to like them.

And that's about it for Lancaster County nut production.

Breweries, Wineries, Pubs

While the "Plain People" generally frown upon alcohol, other citizens have had a more embracing attitude toward "spirits." Late in the 18th century, 62 taverns lined the 68 miles of highway from Lancaster to Philadelphia. They were the centers of public life, hosting meetings, theatrical presentations, and social affairs. On July 3, 1791, Pres. George Washington visited Lancaster and dined at the White Swan Hotel on the square. The following day, he enjoyed an elaborate dinner at the courthouse, where 15 toasts took place, the final one to "the illustrious president of the United States."

In an area that produced as much grain as the Amish Country, it was almost inevitable that the malting of grain would become a popular hobby and an important industry. For a short time, the town of Mount Joy claimed to be "The Malt Capital of the Nation." At one time, the number of distilleries in the area surpassed the number of gristmills—183 to 164.

In later years, many corner bars in Lancaster and other towns had their own breweries on the premises. Rumor has it that during Prohibition, the pipes beneath the city of Lancaster carried beer from clandestine breweries to homes and taverns. Today, several small breweries and wineries operate in the area.

Bube's Brewery, 102 N. Market Street, Mount Joy, 717-653-2056. The oldest Victorian-era brewery still standing in the United States. Tours available by appointment.

Lancaster County Winery, Rawlinsville Road, Willow Street, 717-464-3555. Set on one of Lancaster County's oldest farms. Tours available.

Mount Hope Estate and Winery, PA 72 north of Manheim, close to PA Turnpike exit. Mount Hope is home to the Pennsylvania Renaissance Faire, a re-creation of life in medieval England, held weekends from August through October.

Nissley Vineyards and Winery, Bainbridge-Maytown Road, Bainbridge, 717-426-3514. The winery offers tours, entertainment, and sales of products. In October, the winery hosts a seven-mile road race, which gained fame in 1983 when a cow broke loose and joined the race. Despite a lack of training, she ran well for several miles. However, since she hadn't officially registered, she wasn't eligible for prizes.

Stoudt's Brewery Company, Route 272, Adamstown, 717-484-4387. This microbrewery offers tours and beer tasting. All beer is brewed without preservatives, in accordance with the Bavarian Purity Law of 1516. Brewery Hall offers dancing and entertainment.

Restaurants

Food and frugality are important parts of local culture, and they come together at many local restaurants. When a good Dutchman goes out for a meal, he's more concerned with the food and the cost than with the atmosphere.

Restaurants called smorgasbords focus on food and frugality. For one price, you'll get all the food that you can eat, as well as friendly service, but don't expect strolling violinists. Reservations aren't required, but they can be a good idea in busy seasons.

Many other restaurants offer Pennsylvania Dutch menus, but not the all-you-can-eat option. And, you can now find eating establishments that offer foods of almost every description. If you favor familiar names and tastes, many chains and franchises have outlets in the area.

Pennsylvania Dutch food is a local staple. It developed over the centuries, before foods from all over the world could be shipped in. It featured foods that were locally grown. So, a genuine Pennsylvania Dutch meal had to consist of foods that were available in the area 100 years ago. Locally produced breads, fruits, meats, and vegetables fit that description.

Traditional Pennsylvania Dutch meals tend to be rather high in fat and cholesterol. Plenty of fruits and vegetables are always available, but they don't get top billing on the menu. Slowly, however, more restaurants are adding choices for health-conscious diners. If you can't find what you want on the menu, just ask. Almost every restaurant will accommodate your requests.

"Seven sweets and seven sours" are an important part of the Pennsylvania Dutch custom of overeating. Supposedly, they were on the table for every meal. Many are still local favorites,

Hearty Pennsylvania Dutch food is served family-style at many of the restaurants in the Amish Country. (Courtesy Pennsylvania Dutch Visitors Bureau)

and there's likely to be some variation in restaurants. The original sweets and sours were:

Fox-grape jelly
Apple butter
Strawberry jam
Quince chips
Honey in the comb
Spiced peaches
Ginger pears
Kimmel cherries
Green-tomato pickles
Red beets
Pepper cabbage
Sour beans
Jerusalem artichokes
Chowchow

The following codes in the restaurant list below identify each establishment's price range:

E—Expensive; a complete meal for one is likely to cost more than $20

M—Moderate; a complete meal for one is likely to cost between $10 and $19.99

I—Inexpensive; a complete meal for one is likely to cost less than $10.

American

Beechtree Inn, *E*, 5267 Lincoln Highway East (Route 30), Gap, 717-442-900. A 200-year-old inn with five fireplaces, lots of atmosphere, and a contemporary menu.

The Brownstown Restaurant, *I*, 1 S. Main Street, Brownstown, 717-657-9077. Malcolm Forbes used to ride his motorcycle to Brownstown and dine here.

Cameron Estate Inn & Restaurant, *E*, Donegal Springs Road, Mount Joy, 717-653-1773. Housed in an 1805 mansion, and run by Betty Groff, author of many cookbooks. Offers American and European country dishes.

Center City Grille, *M,* 10 S. Prince Street, Lancaster, 717-299-3456. A comfortable restaurant popular with the young, professional crowd.

The Corn Crib, *I,* Route 41, Christiana, 610-593-2721. It's doubtful that any establishment has a lower sense of self-esteem. Its newspaper ads often use reverse psychology, telling readers they'll be lucky to survive the awful food.

Kreider Dairy Farms Family Restaurants, *I,* 1461 Lancaster Road, Manheim, 717-665-5039, and Centerville Road and Columbia Avenue, Lancaster, 717-393-3410. Dairy favorites such as milk shakes and sundaes are popular at these family-owned eating spots.

Revere Tavern, *M/E,* 3063 Lincoln Highway East (Route 30), Paradise, 717-687-8602. In operation since 1740, specializing in steak and seafood.

Asian

Asian Restaurant, *M,* 553 N. Pine Street, a block from Franklin and Marshall College, Lancaster, 717-397-7095. The menu includes items from many different Asian countries. If the menu indicates that an item is spicy hot, believe it.

British

Quip's Pub, *I,* 457 New Holland Avenue, Lancaster, 717-396-3903. The menu includes fish and chips and the atmosphere features British darts.

Chinese

House of Shanghai, *I/M,* 2126 Lincoln Highway East (Route 30), Lancaster, 717-299-6116.

Wang's, *I/M,* 938 Columbia Avenue, Lancaster, 717-293-1688.

Formal Dining

The Restaurant at Donecker's, *E,* 333 N. State Street, Ephrata, 717-738-9501. Part of the Donecker's complex. Much of the menu is French.

Strawberry Hill, *M,* 128 W. Strawberry Street, Lancaster, 717-392-5544. An eclectic menu offers vegetarian choices and late-night specials.

Windows, *E,* 16 W. King Street, Lancaster, 717-295-1316. Traditional French cuisine and elegant surroundings.

Indian

Kiran Palace, *M,* 1358 Columbia Avenue, Lancaster, in Stone Mill Plaza, 717-295-9508. The tastes, aromas, sounds, and sights of India come to Lancaster. The food is delicious, but tends to be quite spicy. If you don't like spicy-hot foods, ask them to make things mild.

Italian

Italian Villa East, *M,* 2331 Lincoln Highway East (Route 30), Lancaster. Traditional Italian and American dishes share menu space.

Lombardo's, *M,* 216 Harrisburg Avenue, Lancaster, 717-394-3749. Closed Sundays. Lancaster's best-known Italian restaurant is locally famous for spaghetti. Reservations are recommended.

Milano's, *M/E,* 51 N. Market Street, downtown Lancaster, 717-399-9092.

Portofino's, *M/E,* 254 E. Frederick Street, Lancaster, 717-394-1635.

Macrobiotic

Meadows Natural Foods, *M,* 10 Front Street, Lititz, 717-626-7374. Located inside a natural-foods store, a small restaurant offers soup and sandwiches for lunch and takeout meals several nights a week.

Mexican

Carlos & Charlie's, *I,* 915 N. Plum Street, Lancaster, 717-293-8704, and 2309 Columbia Avenue, Lancaster, 717-399-1912.

Pennsylvania Dutch

The Amish Barn Restaurant, *I,* Route 340 between Bird-In-

Hand and Intercourse, 717-768-8886. Pennsylvania Dutch favorites. Quilts on display.

Bird-in-Hand Family Restaurant, *I,* 2760 Old Philadelphia Pike, Bird-In-Hand, 717-768-8266. Family dining, buffets, salad bar.

Family Style Restaurant, *I,* Route 30, 4½ miles east of Lancaster, 717-393-2323. Buffets, kids-eat-free specials.

Good 'N' Plenty, *I,* Route 896, Smoketown, 717-394-7111. Seating for 600+ diners. Hearty family-style dining.

Harvest Drive Restaurant, *M,* Clearview Road, south of Route 340, Intercourse, 717-768-7186. Unusual items such as baked corn and pot pie bring diners back again and again.

Stoltzfus Farm Restaurant, *M,* E. Newport Road (Route 772), Intercourse, 717-768-8156. Closed Sundays. Stoltzfus is one of the most common Amish names. This family-owned restaurant caters to families.

Zinn's Diner, *I,* Route 272 at PA Turnpike exit, Denver, 717-336-2210. More than just a diner, it's a park, a miniature golf course, an arcade, softball fields, and an information center.

Smorgasbords

Hershey Farm Restaurant, *M,* Route 896, Strasburg, 717-687-8635. Traditional Pennsylvania Dutch menu features seven sweets and seven sours.

Miller's Smorgasbord/Country Fare Restaurant, *I/M,* Route 30 at Ronks Road, five miles east of Lancaster, 717-687-6621. If you'd play a word association game with Lancaster County residents, the most common reaction to "smorgasbord" would be "Miller's." For decades, it's been a popular eating spot. Country Fare Restaurant offers farm-fresh breakfasts, deli sandwiches, and much more good eating.

Shady Maple, *I,* Route 23 east of Blue Ball, 717-354-8222. Closed Sundays. This popular eating spot and grocery store attracts diners and shoppers from three counties.

Willow Valley, *M,* three miles south of Lancaster on Route 222. Part of the Willow Valley complex, the smorgasbord offers three meals a day, seven days a week.

Unusual Dining Atmospheres

These establishments place equal emphasis on the surroundings and the food, allowing you to dine in a catacomb, for instance, or a train car.

Bube's Brewery & Catacombs Restaurant, *M/E,* 102 N. Market Street, Mount Joy, 717-653-2056. Come on down! The Catacombs is 40 feet underground. Reservations highly recommended.

The Clermont Cafe, *I,* Route 30 and Route 896, east of Lancaster, 717-392-5557. Located in the Fulton Steamboat Inn, and named after the first successful passenger steamship, which Lancaster County native Robert Fulton built.

The Horse Inn, *M,* 200 block of N. Marshall Street, Lancaster, 717-392-5580. It's actually located in an alley, but it's not hard to find. The "booths" are authentic horse stalls.

Red Caboose Restaurant, *I/M,* 312A Paradise Lane, just east of the Strasburg Railroad terminal, Strasburg, 717-687-5001. Eat in Victorian-era dining coaches. Menu features many Pennsylvania Dutch dishes. At the same site is a motel whose rooms are actual cabooses.

Vietnamese

Lanvina's, *I,* 1651 Lincoln Highway East (Route 462), Lancaster, 717-399-0199, and 1762 Columbia Avenue, Lancaster, 717-393-7748. Perhaps the best dining bargain in town. Few diners can eat everything on their plate. Almost everybody winds up taking something home.

Where the Locals Gather

When the local folks want to dine casually, and perhaps watch the "Big Game," these are some favorite haunts.

The Barn Door, *I,* 14 Blue Rock Road, Millersville, 717-872-9943.

Blue Ball Hotel, *I,* Routes 23 and 322, Blue Ball, 717-354-9006.

Downtown Sports Lounge, *I,* 227 N. Prince Street, Lancaster, 717-291-9222.

Fulton Bar, *I*, 637 N. Plum Street, Lancaster, 717-291-1098.

Hilltop Inn, *I*, 415 E. Main Street, Ephrata, 717-733-6331.

Lancaster Dispensing Company, *I*, 33 N. Market Street (beside Central Market), Lancaster, 717-299-4602.

Market Fare Restaurant, *I*, Grant and Market (beside Central Market), Lancaster, 717-299-7090.

Rawlinsville Hotel, *I*, 3 Drytown Road, Rawlinsville, 717-284-4967.

Rising Sun Hotel, *I*, 518 Cherry Street, Columbia, 717-684-9991.

White Horse Inn, *I*, 5589 Old Philadelphia Pike (Route 340), Gap, 717-768-9028.

Self-Guided Tours

If you enjoy exploring, here are several routes that will give you good looks at the scenery and other interesting sights.

Heart of the Amish Country
(For cars and bikes) 17 miles, basically flat terrain

Begin at the Bird-In-Hand Farmer's Market on Route 340.
At the west end of the parking lot, go left on Maple Avenue.
Go right on North Ronks Road.
Go left onto Irishtown Road.
Go left on Old Leacock Road.
Go left on Harvest/South Harvest Road.
Go right on Old Philadelphia Pike.
Go left on North Harvest Road.
At stop sign, go straight onto Newport Road.
Go left on Scenic Road.
Go right and quickly left, staying on Scenic Road.
Go left on Centerville Road.
Go left on Zelternich Road.
Go right on Musser School Road.
Go left on Groffdale Road.
Go right on East Eby Road.
Go left on Stumptown Road.
Go left on Monterey Road.
Go left to Miller's store.
Return to Monterey Road and go left.

Go right on Church Road.
Go left on Beechdale Road.
Go left on Old Philadelphia Pike.
Turn right into parking lot.

What You'll See: On the roads that you'll travel, one **Amish farm** runs into another. On many farms, you'll see signs advertising various items made there, such as **quilts and furniture.** The Gordonville Fire Company is home to very popular sales of quilts and **buggies.**

At the intersection of Stumptown and Newport, there's a little **park** beside the creek. At the same intersection is **Mascot Roller Mill.** From May through October, you can see corn ground into flour.

Miller's is a natural-foods store on an Amish farm. Prices there are considerably lower than in a traditional store.

Lancaster County Covered Bridges

(For cars and reasonably strong bicyclists) 33 miles, hilly terrain

Begin at Lititz Springs Park, on Route 501, beside the railroad tracks, in Lititz.
Go left onto North Broad Street.
Go right on East Front Street.
Go left on North Cedar Street.
Go left on North Water Street.
Go right on Newport Road.
Go left on Orchard Road.
Go left on Clay Road.
Go right on Carpenter Road.
Go straight onto Lincoln Road.
Go right on Brubaker Road.
Go right on Middle Creek Road.
Go right on Erb's Bridge Road.
Go through Erb's Covered Bridge.
Go right on Main Street in Rothsville.
Go quickly left on Church Street.
Go left on Log Cabin Road.
Go through Rose Hill Covered Bridge.

Go left on Rose Hill Road.
Go right on Zook's Mill Road.
Go left on Industrial Road.
Go right on Newport Road.
Go left on Main Street in Brownstown.
Go right on Turtle Hill Road.
Go left on High Road.
Go right on Metzler Road.
Go left on West Farmersville Road.
Go right on Metzler Road.
Go right on Pashing Weeg.*
Go right on Cider Mill Road.
Go through Eberly's Mill Covered Bridge.
Go right on Covered Bridge Road.
Go left on Farmersville Road.
Go right on West Farmersville Road.
Go left on Brethren Church Road.
Go right on Center Square Road.
Go right on Quarry Road.
Go left on Pinetown Road.
Go left on Bridge Road.
Go through Pinetown Covered Bridge.
Go right on Mondale Road.
Go right on Hunsecker Road.
Go through Hunsecker Covered Bridge.
Go right on Butter Road.
Butter Road becomes Creek Road.
Cross Route 272.
Go right on Oregon Road.
Go immediately left on Creek Road.
Go left on Millport Road.
Go right on Owl Hill Road.
Go right on Kissel Hill Road.
Go right on Locust Street.
Go left on Main Street.
Go right on North Broad Street and return to the park.
What You'll See: This tour will take you through five of

Lancaster County's covered bridges. The **Hunsecker bridge** is the oldest in the county—but not really. A covered bridge has been at that site since 1843, but the current structure dates only to 1975. The original bridge floated away in the flood waters of Hurricane Agnes in 1972.

That same storm washed the **Pinetown bridge** downstream. Work crews then moved it back where it belongs.

Also on this tour, you'll begin in the pleasant town of **Lititz,** home to the world's oldest pretzel bakery, and a chocolate factory.

In **Rothsville,** polo matches take place on Sunday afternoons in summer. Just before the first covered bridge is an excellent produce stand.

*Pashing Weeg is Pennsylvania Dutch. Several roads in that immediate area have street signs in Pennsylvania Dutch.

Down by the River
(For cars and experienced bikers) 30 miles, very difficult climbs

Begin at the junction of PA 999 and PA 441 in Washington Boro, about three miles south of Columbia.

Go south on River Road.

Stay on River Road until you see a sign that points you to the Holtwood Pinnacle.

Go right on Pinnacle Road.

Note: Be careful of the road signs. River Road isn't exactly straight.

What You'll See: After you get to the end of Pinnacle Road, you can get out and walk. You'll come to the **Pinnacle,** which provides a great view of the **Susquehanna River,** 537 feet below. If you're the adventurous type, there are trails that will take you down to the bottom. Or, you can have a picnic in the little park at the top. Then, just reverse your course.

Lancaster City Tour
(For pedestrians) 1.5 miles, moderate terrain

Begin at Penn Square, at the intersection of King and Queen streets.

Go west on King and north on Prince.
Go west on Chestnut.
Go north on Charlotte.
Go east on Lemon.
Go south on Duke.
Go west on Orange.
Go south on Queen.

What You'll See: This easy walk will take you through the business district and residential neighborhoods. On the square is **Central Market,** the oldest publicly owned market in the country. It's open Tuesday, Friday, and Saturday. On Prince Street is the **Fulton Opera House.**

On Charlotte Street you'll see some beautiful older **homes.** On Lemon Street is the **Northwest Corridor Park.** Opened in 1994, this linear park was once a railroad bed.

At the intersection of Duke and Orange is **Saint James Episcopal Church,** one of Lancaster's oldest and most beautiful. Half a block away, on East Orange Street, is **First Reformed Church,** another old and beautiful structure.

Covered Bridges

As you travel through the Amish Country, you'll have opportunities to see many functioning reminders of the past. One of the most visible, and most popular, is the covered bridge. At one time, many bridges had covers on them. Although they look very pretty, the purpose of the covers is purely practical—to protect the roadbed from the elements. Exposed to rain, snow, and sun, a wooden roadbed would quickly wear out and become dangerous, lasting only 15 to 20 years. Under cover, it lasts a long time, perhaps a century.

A common perception associates covered bridges with Vermont and Indiana, but the structures had their American beginnings in Pennsylvania. The first one spanned the Schuylkill in Philadelphia, and many covered-bridge enthusiasts are surprised to learn that one covered bridge still stands within the city of Philadelphia. It's used for pedestrian and horse traffic across the Wissahickon Creek in Fairmount Park.

The longest covered bridge ever built connected Columbia in Lancaster County and Wrightsville in York County. Spanning the wide Susquehanna River, it measured 5,690 feet, well over a mile. It met its final demise when soldiers burned it during the Civil War.

Today, covered bridges are still fairly numerous in Pennsylvania. The commonwealth's 1991 total of 226 was the highest in the nation. At one time, 64 of Pennsylvania's counties had at least one covered bridge. Lancaster County has more (30,

Pennsylvania has more covered bridges than any other state. (Courtesy Pennsylvania Dutch Visitors Bureau)

including two that link Lancaster and Chester counties) than any other county. That number was much higher before Hurricane Agnes struck in 1972.

Of the 30 covered bridges in Lancaster County, 23 still carry vehicular traffic. The others are either tourist attractions, privately owned, or used just for pedestrian traffic.

While covered bridges are definitely an endangered species, the ones in Lancaster County appear to have a fairly secure future. A strong preservationist sentiment surrounds them, and Lancaster County has a highway crew that devotes most of its efforts to maintaining the covered bridges. It may be the only such crew in the country. Still, it's impossible to save some bridges, but there's no law against building a new one, and Lancaster County did build a new covered bridge in the 1990s. It's the Colmanville Bridge in southwestern Lancaster County, near Pequea. The original structure was in such bad condition that it was beyond repair, so a new bridge went up right next to it.

If you've never been through a covered bridge, you should know a few things about them. First, they're wide enough for only one car, or one buggy. A common building requirement was that a bridge had to be high and wide enough for a wagonload of hay. Before you enter, be certain that nothing is coming in the opposite direction. Also, the ride is bumpy, so it's wise to go slowly. In addition, covered bridges have low weight limits. Five tons is the usual limit, and height restrictions are commonly 11 feet, or 11 feet, six inches. You'll be fine in a car, van, or small truck, but RVs will have to find another route.

If you want to take pictures, pull a good distance away from the bridge. If somebody tells you that George Washington rode through a particular bridge, remember that Washington died six years before the first bridge opened.

According to tradition, couples travelling through a covered bridge will enjoy good fortune if they kiss inside.

Where to Find Them

Since they can't handle heavy traffic, the remaining covered bridges are on country roads, and many are difficult to find.

Here are some that are relatively easy to locate.

Paradise/Leaman Place Bridge, eastern Lancaster County, in the heart of Amish farm country. From U.S. Route 30 in Paradise, turn north on Belmont Road. The bridge is about a mile straight ahead, and a plaque details its history. In the 1980s a truck tried to go through, and knocked the bridge off its foundation. The county restored the bridge (and prosecuted the truck driver).

Landis Mill Bridge, central Lancaster County, adjacent to Park City Shopping Center. To find this bridge, go west from Lancaster on Harrisburg Pike. When you see Park City Shopping Center on your right, go past the center and turn right on Plaza Boulevard. Then, go to the next road on your left. You'll see the bridge. Once, this area was the Landis farm, and a much quieter place than it is now.

Herr's Mill Bridge, eastern Lancaster County. From U.S. Route 30, go south on Ronks Road. This may be the best bridge for exploring. It's now a tourist attraction, and closed to motor vehicles. It's also the only two-span bridge left within the county.

Kurtz's Mill Bridge, in Lancaster County Central Park. From downtown Lancaster, go south on Duke Street. After you cross the Conestoga River, make the second right, Eshelman Mill Road. Go about a quarter of a mile and turn right on Golf Road. At the bottom of the hill, stay to the left, and the bridge is straight ahead. This bridge wasn't always here. It originally spanned the Conestoga River in northeastern Lancaster County. Hurricane Agnes in 1972 washed it off its foundation, and it found a new home in the park. You can walk under this one and examine the building techniques.

Hunsecker Bridge, about five miles north of Lancaster. From Lancaster, go north on PA 272. After you pass the Landis Valley Farm Museum, turn right on Hunsecker Road. It's about two miles to the bridge, which is the longest bridge entirely in Lancaster County, and a relative youngster, built in 1975 to replace the original, which Hurricane Agnes washed away.

Kauffman's Distillery Bridge, west of Manheim. From Manheim, go west on PA 772. Turn left on West Sunhill Road. The bridge is right there. It's in a picturesque setting, and horses frequently graze right under it.

Baumgardner's Mill Bridge, southern Lancaster County, near Willow Street. From Lancaster, go south on PA 272. South of Willow Street, turn right on Byerland Church Road. It's about two miles to the bridge. Rebuilt in 1987, this bridge is in excellent condition.

Forry's Mill Bridge, western Lancaster County. From Lancaster go west on PA 23. About three miles east of Marietta, you'll see a housing development called Bridge Valley. Turn right on Bridge Valley Road, and the bridge is directly ahead of you. In fact, it's visible from PA 23.

The best way to locate all of Lancaster County's covered bridges is to buy a road map that shows them all.

For more information on covered bridges in Pennsylvania and around the world, contact the Theodore Burr Covered Bridge Society, P.O. Box 2383, Lancaster, PA 17603-2383.

For further reading, see *Pennsylvania's Covered Bridges,* Benjamin D. and June R. Landis, University of Pittsburgh Press.

The winter holiday season finds farmer's markets in the area brimming with colorful poinsettias as well as Pennsylvania Dutch foods. (Courtesy Pennsylvania Dutch Visitors Bureau)

Farmer's Markets and Roadside Stands

Farmer's Markets

In earlier days, farmer's markets provided an important medium for moving foods from the farm to city dwellers. With the growth of supermarkets, the number of farmer's markets has decreased, but those that still function are quite popular, and economically viable. They allow farmers to sell their goods directly to the consumer. Frequently, the produce you buy has just come from the field. In addition, farmer's markets create a friendlier and more personal atmosphere than you can expect to find in a supermarket. Often, the person selling you an item has actually grown it or baked it, so you can find out exactly what's in it.

In the Amish Country, markets of many descriptions are important parts of the culture and the economy.

Bird-In-Hand Farmer's Market, Route 340, Bird-In-Hand, 717-393-9674. Open Friday and Saturday all year. Also Wednesday from April to November and Thursday from July to October.

Central Market, Penn Square, downtown Lancaster, 717-291-4739. Open Tuesday, Friday, and Saturday all year. This is the country's oldest publicly owned farmer's market, selling produce, baked goods, and a wide variety of ethnic foods. With a purchase, you will receive an hour of free parking at the nearby Prince Street Garage.

Columbia Market House, Third Street, Columbia. Open Friday and Saturday.

115

Donecker's Farmer's Market, 100 N. State Street, Ephrata, 717-738-9503. Open Thursday, Friday, and Saturday.

Downington Farmer's Market, Route 30 East, 610-269-4050.

Green Dragon Market, North State Street, Ephrata, 717-738-1117. You'll find food and much more here. Open Fridays only.

Meadowbrook Farmer's Market, Route 23, Leola, 717-656-2226.

Root's Country Market, Graystone Road, south of Manheim, 717-898-7811. Like the Green Dragon, Root's has almost everything for sale. Open Tuesdays only.

Roadside Stands

You'll see roadside stands all over the Amish Country. In many instances, they'll give you better prices than stores because they eliminate the middlemen. It's not just the Amish who operate these stands. Anybody with something to sell is likely to set up a table in the front yard. In suburban neighborhoods, you can find corn and tomatoes fresh from the back yard on sale in the front yard.

Many of these stands are seasonal, selling primarily fresh produce. Others are open all year (but never on Sunday), and sell baked goods, quilts, and crafts.

Sometimes, the stands really aren't stands. Sometimes, they're wagon loaded with freshly picked produce and parked by the side of the road. Freshness is an obvious appeal of roadside stands. Produce has probably come directly from the field, and baked goods may still be warm.

Many local people like to go for a drive in the country and stock up at a favorite farm stand. The stands are on highways and on the backroads. PA 340 is home to a good number of stands. Route 322 near New Holland and Ephrata has acquired the nickname of "Cantaloupe Alley" because it's in a region where farmers grow lots of melons, and in August their wagons often overflow. Here are the locations of a few good stands.

Countryside Road Stand, Stumptown Road, Upper Leacock Township. From PA 772, northwest of Intercourse, turn north on Stumptown Road. The stand is on an Amish farm about half

The Green Dragon Market. (Courtesy Pennsylvania Dutch Visitors Bureau)

Hay auction at the Green Dragon Market. (Courtesy Pennsylvania Dutch Visitors Bureau)

a mile up the road. It features produce, baked goods, quilts, and homemade root beer by the cup or gallon jug. On a hot day, it's a great thirst fighter.

Fisher's Produce and Quilts, Route 741, between Strasburg and Gap. This is an excellent source of corn, melons, and baked goods. Local residents (including the author) heading to the beaches frequently stop here to stock up.

Hoover's Fruit and Vegetable Farm, Erb's Bridge Road, Ephrata Township. From PA 772 in Rothsville, turn north on Picnic Woods Road. Go through the covered bridge, and the road becomes Covered Bridge Road. The stand is a few hundred feet ahead, and features produce from a large fruit and vegetable farm.

Attractions

The Amish Farm and House, 2395 Lincoln Highway East (Route 30), Lancaster, 717-394-6185. A guided tour through the large farm and house explains the Amish way of life. The operating farm has a variety of animals. Open daily.

The Amish Village, Route 896, two miles north of Strasburg, 717-687-8511. Most of the important parts of Amish life are here—a house, a one-room school, a smokehouse, a blacksmith shop, and farm animals. You'll also find a picnic area and a gift shop. Open daily.

Donecker's, 100 N. State Street, Ephrata, 717-738-9500. This complex includes The Artworks, The Fashion Store, The Restaurant, The Inns, and The Farmer's Market. You can eat, shop, and sleep here.

Dutch Wonderland, 2249 Lincoln Highway East (Route 30), Lancaster, 717-291-1888. See how the Amish really spend their days—riding roller coasters and eating cotton candy! (Just kidding, of course.) This is an amusement park with a monorail and boat rides.

Eagle Falls Adventure Park, 2423 Lincoln Highway East (Route 30), Lancaster, 717-397-4674. Water slides and miniature golf, arcades and ice-cream parlor.

Ephrata Cloister, Routes 272 and 322, Ephrata, 717-733-6600. This was the home of an 18th-century religious communal society. Restored buildings display the austere lifestyle.

Folk Craft Center & Museum, 441 Mount Sidney Road, Wit-

To depict 18th-century monastic life at the Ephrata Cloister, actors present the drama Vorspiel during the summer. (Courtesy Pennsylvania Dutch Visitors Bureau)

mer, just north of Route 340, 717-397-3609. Craft shops, Americana/Pennsylvania Dutch museum, herb-garden tours.

Gettysburg Battlefield, Gettysburg, 717-334-1124. The site of the bloodiest and most famous military battle in the history of North America. From July 1 to July 3, Union and Confederate soldiers fought and died. The battlefield has been preserved to look much as it did when the fighting ended. Today, the battlefield is a peaceful place. It's ideal for bicycling, and perhaps at its peak of beauty in late April when the dogwoods are blooming.

Hanover Shoe Farms, Route 194 South, Hanover, southwestern York County, 717-637-8931. The world's largest breeder of Standardbred (trotters and pacers) horses.

HersheyPark, Hershey's Chocolate World, Hershey, 800-HERSHEY. HersheyPark is a famous amusement park in Chocolatetown that offers rides, entertainment, games, etc. Open daily in summer, weekends in spring and fall. Chocolate World shows how chocolate comes into existence. Open all year.

Kitchen Kettle Village, Route 340, Intercourse, 717-768-8261 or 800-732-3538. A collection of 30 shops where craftspeople produce baskets, furniture, and food. Closed Sundays.

Living Waters Museum, Route 896, south of Route 30, Strasburg, 717-687-7854. Light, water, and sound combine to produce "Liquid Fireworks."

Mill Bridge Village, South Ronks Road, Strasburg, fi mile south of Route 30, 717-687-8181 or 800-MIL-BRIG. Home of Lancaster County's longest covered bridge, Mill Bridge Village offers shops, craft demonstrations, entertainment, food, and a camping resort.

Pennsylvania Renaissance Faire, Mount Hope Estate and Winery, Route 72 north of Manheim at Pennsylvania Turnpike, 717-665-7021. A re-creation of medieval England features jousts, costumed entertainers, food, and crafts of the era. Open Saturday, Sunday, and Monday from late June through Labor Day, Saturday and Sunday in September and October.

The People's Place, Route 340, Intercourse, 717-768-7171. The People's Place offers an in-depth and straightforward look at Amish and Mennonite life. With exhibits and films, it explains why they live as they do, and clears up many misconceptions. Closed Sundays.

Sight and Sound Entertainment Centre, Route 896, south of Route 30, Strasburg, 717-687-7800. "The Nation's Largest Christian Theatre" features has 1,400 seats, and puts on live shows.

Strasburg Railroad, Route 741, east of Strasburg, 717-687-7522. America's oldest short line railroad takes visitors on a steam-powered journey through Amish farmlands. The Railroad Museum of Pennsylvania is across the highway.

Wax Museum of Lancaster County, 2249 Lincoln Highway East (Route 30), Lancaster, 717-393-3679. Lifelike animated features take visitors through Lancaster County history.

Weavertown One-Room School, Route 340 east of Bird-In-Hand, 717-768-3976. Lifelike animation re-creates a school day in a one-room schoolhouse. Open daily Easter through Thanksgiving.

Jacob Zook's Hex & Craft Shops, Route 30 East, Paradise, 717-687-6333. Hex signs decorate many barns in the region. Learn about them and purchase your own.

For Rainy Days

One major advantage of a vacation in the Amish Country is that it's not really dependent on good weather. Unlike a trip to the beach, you don't need sunshine and warm temperatures to enjoy a trip to Lancaster County. Even on rainy days, you can do most of the things that visitors normally do. You can go to **restaurants** and **museums.** You can ride the **rails,** and you can do some **shopping.**

The best advice is that rainy weather won't ruin a vacation in the Amish Country.

For Children

The Amish Country has plenty of attractions that will keep the younger set happy. **Dutch Wonderland, Eagle Falls Adventure Park,** and **HersheyPark** will appeal to almost everyone, as will a ride on the **Strasburg Railroad.**

The Strasburg Railroad. (Courtesy Pennsylvania Dutch Visitors Bureau)

Conestoga wagon.

At **Sturgis Pretzels,** children can test their skill at twisting pretzels. At **Candy Americana** in Lititz and at **Hershey's Chocolate World,** they can see how raw materials become candy, and at **Herr's Chips** in Nottingham, they can see how potatoes become chips (see Museums and Food chapters). They can play miniature golf, and they can eat.

Along the way, children can pick up some interesting information to impress their friends. They can go back to school and tell everyone that the Kentucky rifle came from Pennsylvania, and that the Conestoga wagon came from Lancaster County.

For Rail and River Fans

Riding the Rails

If you like trains, the Amish Country is an excellent place to visit. You can take Amtrak to Harrisburg, Lancaster, and Coatesville. The Amtrak line passes right through the agricultural heart of the Amish Country in Chester and Lancaster counties.

In the area, you'll find many tourist railroads. In Strasburg are the Railroad Museum of Pennsylvania and the Red Caboose Motel, where all the rooms are real cabooses. Here's a list of the tourist railroads in the area.

Blue Mountain & Reading Railroad, Route 61, north of Reading, 215-562-4083.

Gettysburg Railroad, Constitution Avenue, Gettysburg, 717-334-6932.

Middletown & Hummelstown Railroad, 170 Brown Street, Middletown, 717-944-4435.

Strasburg Railroad, Route 741, Strasburg, 717-687-7522.

WK & S Railroad, Kempton (Berks County), 215-756-6469.

The Amtrak station in Lancaster is at the intersection of North Queen Street and McGovern Avenue, on the north end of town (717-291-5080).

If you like to snap pictures of trains, the Strasburg Railroad is excellent. It moves rather slowly, and crosses a number of roads that provide good angles. Amtrak trains zoom past

Irishtown Road near Bird-In-Hand. A major Conrail line runs beside Route 441 between Columbia and Washington Boro. It supplies excellent photo opportunities. You can get a great view of freight operations from a pedestrian bridge across the tracks beside Harrisburg Pike in Lancaster.The bridge is just across the street from the football field at Franklin and Marshall College.

Down by the River

While most of the Amish Country is rolling hills and farms, the area along the Susquehanna River has a distinctively different topography. The River Hills are steep and much more difficult to farm. Much of the area from Three Mile Island to the Maryland line is wooded and quite hilly. It's a favorite spot for many kinds of outdoor recreation, and there are a few Amish farms in the area.

The Susquehanna is no good for transporting freight, but recreational boaters like it. Swimmers occasionally venture in, but it's a dangerous river. It's rocky and the currents are very tricky. Just about every year, it claims several lives. The best advice concerning swimming in the Susquehanna is *don't!*

The steep cliffs along the river and the islands in it provide excellent nesting places for birds of prey. Hawks and ospreys are fairly common sights, and in recent years some bald eagles have moved in.

Among local residents, **tubing** (floating down the creek in a big inner tube) in the Pequea Creek is a popular summer pastime. Tubing expeditions are available at **Sickman's Mill** on Sandhill Road in Conestoga, 717-872-5951.

Several undeveloped areas along the river are excellent for observing nature. **Kelly's Run Gorge** near Holtwood has sheer rock vertical walls, with ferns and wild flowers growing. **Fernglen,** near Susquehannock State Park, has lots of ferns. The **Holtwood Pinnacle,** on Pinnacle Road, offers a great view of the river and it's so high that you can't hear the motors on boats.

Public boat launches are available at Pequea, on Route 324, at Peach Bottom, at Bainbridge, and at Middletown on the eastern side of the river. On the western side, Goldsboro and Long Level in York County provide access for boaters.

The Susquehanna is a wide river, more than a mile across in places. It begins life as a narrow stream in Cooperstown, New York, just down the street from the Baseball Hall of Fame. It empties into the Chesapeake Bay at Havre de Grace, Maryland.

The most famous, or notorious, place on the river is **Three Mile Island,** home of the nuclear power plant that almost melted down in 1979. Three Mile Island is in the river in Dauphin County, just north of the Lancaster County line. A visitor's center on Route 441 explains everything that happened in the accident.

About 10 miles upstream from Three Mile Island is **Harrisburg,** the capital of Pennsylvania. Farther north, at Millersburg, is a **ferry.** It's not a tourist attraction. It's a regular, working ferry. It continues to operate because there aren't many bridges across the wide river. In fact, no bridges cross the river between Duncannon and Sunbury, a stretch of about 50 miles.

Sometimes, it's nice to sit and watch the river flow. One fine spot for river watching is the **community park** in Washington Boro in Lancaster County, at the intersection of PA 999 and PA 441. For much of its length, Route 441 stays within sight of the river.

Museums, Historic Sights, and Churches

History and tradition are large parts of life in the Amish Country. As you can see at these museums, the Amish are only a part of the area's history. These museums record the history of people, nature, trains, steam engines, and agriculture. The days and hours of operation vary from season to season and from year to year, so check ahead to make sure that a particular museum is open when you're visiting.

American Military Edged Weaponry Museum, 3562 Old Philadelphia Pike (PA 340), Intercourse, 717-768-7185. Admission charge. A collection of knives, swords, bayonets, and memorabilia from all periods of American military history.

Archives Museum, 200 block of East Main Street, Lititz, on the Moravian Congregation grounds, 717-626-8515. Admission charge. Documents, furniture, implements, and musical instruments from the early days of Lititz.

Brandywine River Museum, Route 1, Chadds Ford, 215-388-7601. Art of Brandywine region, including Wyeth family paintings.

Candy Americana, in the Wilbur Chocolate Factory, 48 N. Broad Street (PA 501), Lititz, 717-626-1131. Free. A history of candy making, with a focus on chocolate. There's also a small working kitchen where candy is still produced.

Dauphin County Historical Society, 219 S. Front Street, Harrisburg, 717-233-3462. Covers the history of Harrisburg and surrounding areas.

Eicher Indian Museum, in Eicher Sisters' Cabin in Ephrata

Community Park, 717-738-3084 or 717-733-2165. Free. Offers a display of Indian artifacts from all parts of the country.

Gast Classic Motorcars, Route 896, Strasburg, 717-687-0500. Admission charge. An extensive collection of antique, classic, and sports cars, all in mint condition.

Harley Davidson Museum, 1425 Eden Road, York, 717-848-1177. A history of America's favorite motorcycles, which are produced in York.

Heritage Center of Lancaster County, Penn Square, Lancaster, 717-299-6440. Decorative arts, furniture, quilts, rifles, etc. produced by early Lancaster County craftspeople.

Hershey Museum of American Life, Hershey, 717-534-3439. Collection of Pennsylvania German artifacts, Milton Hershey exhibit.

Historical Society of Reading, 940 Center Avenue, Reading, 215-375-4375. Records the history of life in Berks County, with exhibits devoted to railroads, baseball, quilts, and more.

Bob Hoffman's Weightlifting and Softball Hall of Fame, 3300 Board Road, York, 717-767-6481.

Indian Steps Museum, RD 1, Airville, 717-862-3948. Focuses on the history of Indians in the area.

Lancaster County Historical Society, 230 N. President Avenue, Lancaster, beside Wheatland, 717-392-4633. Some parts free, charge for library. A collection of books, documents, and artifacts from more than 250 years of Lancaster County history.

Lancaster Newspapers Newseum, 28 S. Queen Street, Lancaster, 717-291-8600. Free. Visible from the street, it records the history of newspapers and displays many important front pages.

Landis Valley Museum, Oregon Pike (PA 272), Lancaster, 717-569-0401. Admission charge. A large display of early Pennsylvania German rural life, including many pieces of early farm equipment. Gift shop and many special events.

Mushroom Museum at Phillips Place, U.S. Route 1, Kennett Square, 215-388-6082. Admission charge. Exhibits explain the history and mystique of mushrooms.

National Watch and Clock Museum, 514 Poplar Street, Columbia, 717-684-8261. Admission charge, but free for members of National Association of Watch and Clock Collectors. A collection of more than 6,000 timepieces dating from the 1600s to the present. Also, a display of antique music boxes.

National Wax Museum of Lancaster County Heritage, 2249 Route 30 East, Lancaster, 717-393-3679. Admission charge. More than 130 wax figures recreate the history of Lancaster County.

North Museum and Planetarium, College and Buchanan avenues, Lancaster, 717-291-3941. Free. A display of natural history, geology, and archaeology.

People's Place Quilt Museum, Main Street, Intercourse, on the second floor of the Old Country Store, 717-768-7171. This museum houses the first permanent exhibit of antique Amish quilts.

Railroad Museum of Pennsylvania, Route 741 East of Strasburg, 717-687-8628. Admission charge. A large collection of rolling stock, railroad memorabilia, and locomotives from 150 years of railroads in Pennsylvania.

Rough and Tumble Museum, Route 30, Kinzers, 717-442-4249. A large collection of antique steam and gas engines and tractors.

Toy Train Museum, Paradise Lane, Strasburg, just north of Route 741, 717-687-8976. Admission charge. A large display of toy trains dating from 1880, with operating layouts.

Historic Homes

Daniel Boone Homestead, Daniel Boone Road, north of Route 422, Birdsboro, 215-582-4900. Birthplace and homestead of the famous pioneer.

Ellicott House, 123 N. Prince Street, Lancaster. Free. This 18th-century Georgian home now houses the Historic Preservation Trust of Lancaster.

Robert Fulton House, Route 222, south of Quarryville, 717-548-2679. The birthplace of the man credited with inventing the steam engine.

The monumental 1877 Engle Clock, an apostolic clock with 48 moving figures, chimes every day at the National Watch and Clock Museum in Columbia. (Courtesy Pennsylvania Dutch Visitors Bureau)

Steam traction engines like this "Peerless" were a common sight at harvest time in years gone by. Now, however, they operate mainly for the enjoyment of visitors at the Rough and Tumble Museum.
(Courtesy Pennsylvania Dutch Country)

Hans Herr House. (Courtesy Pennsylvania Dutch Visitors Bureau)

Rock Ford Plantation. (Courtesy Pennsylvania Dutch Visitors Bureau)

Hans Herr House, 1849 Hans Herr Drive, Willow Street, 717-464-4438. Admission charge. Lancaster County's oldest building, the home of one of the earliest Mennonite settlers. Includes an outdoor complex with a display of agricultural tools.

Rock Ford Plantation and Kauffman Museum, 881 Rock Ford Road, in Lancaster County Central Park, 717-392-7223. Admission charge. Georgian-style home of Gen. Edward Hand, a Lancastrian who was adjutant general under George Washington.

Wheatland, 1120 Marietta Avenue (PA 23), Lancaster, 717-392-8721. Admission charge. The restored 19th-century home of James Buchanan, Pennsylvania's only president. Guides wear period costumes.

Wright's Ferry Mansion, 38 S. Second Street, Columbia, 717-684-4325. Admission charge. Former home of Susanna Wright, a Quaker who helped to establish colonial self-sufficiency. Houses a collection of early Pennsylvania furniture.

Churches

The Amish Country is like a northern branch office of the Bible Belt. Churches are everywhere, on city streets and country roads. Most are Protestant, and just about every denomination has a church in the area.

Visitors are always welcome at church services, and many churches post messages encouraging visitors to join them. "Visitors Expected" appeared outside one Lancaster church in 1991.

Several churches are among the area's most historic buildings:

Saint James Episcopal, at the corner of East Orange and North Duke streets in Lancaster.

Trinity Lutheran, 31 S. Duke Street, Lancaster.

For Worshippers

To find a complete listing of churches and their service times, check the *Lancaster New Era* on Friday evening or the Lancaster *Intelligencer Journal* on Saturday morning.

James Buchanan.

Wheatland.

The **Lancaster County Council of Churches,** 447 E. King Street, Lancaster, 717-291-2261, can provide further information.

Here are addresses for some denominations:

Roman Catholic

Saint Anthony's, 501 E. Orange Street, Lancaster, 717-394-0669.

Sacred Heart, 558 W. Walnut Street, Lancaster, 717-394-3589.

Mennonite

Mellinger's Mennonite, 1916 Lincoln Highway East (PA 462), Lancaster, 717-397-9360.

Landis Valley Mennonite, 2420 Kissel Hill Road, Lancaster, 717-569-6051.

Lutheran

Grace Lutheran, 517 N. Queen Street, Lancaster, 717-397-2748.

Latter-Day Saints

Church of Jesus Christ, 1200 E. King Street, Lancaster, 717-295-1719.

Methodist

Bird-In-Hand United Methodist, 2612 Old Philadelphia Pike (PA 340), 717-393-7895.

Galleries, Crafts, and Antiques

Art Galleries

Amishland Prints, 3460 Old Philadelphia Pike, Intercourse, 717-768-7273. Original etchings capture the Amish in their daily lives.

Central Market Art Company, 15 W. King Street, Lancaster, 717-392-4466. An outlet for works by Lancaster County artists.

Chadds Ford Gallery, Routes 1 and 100, Chadds Ford, 215-459-5510. To the east of the Amish Country is the home base of the Wyeth family. Near Longwood Gardens and the Brandywine Battlefield, this gallery has the largest Wyeth collection anywhere.

Community Gallery of Lancaster, 135 N. Lime Street, 717-394-3947. This is a member-supported organization that features works by both local artists and internationally known artists such as Renoir and Wyeth. There are also painting and drawing classes for children. Famous artists occasionally stop by for lunch.

Huddle Images, 555 Greenfield Road, Lancaster, 717-295-7456. Photographic scenes of Lancaster County.

Lancaster Graphics, 34 N. Water Street, Lancaster, 717-397-5552. This gallery offers many photographic collections of life in Lancaster County. A very popular one shows all 30 of Lancaster County's covered bridges.

Tremellen Gallery, 114 E. Chestnut Street, Lancaster, 717-392-5339. Original and commissioned works.

An Amish quilt.

A quilting bee. (Courtesy Pennsylvania Dutch Visitors Bureau)

Quilts

As you drive through the Amish Country, you'll see signs that say simply, "Quilts." Amish quilts have become extremely popular among non-Amish. An antique Amish quilt (made before 1950) represents one of the rarest and most popular forms of folk art in North America.

The first quilts were purely practical creations. They were a way of using the leftover pieces of fabric that remained after making clothes. Over the years, quilts acquired greater dignity and, when the textile industry developed in North America, quilters began to use new materials.

Each quilt requires a staggering amount of work. Nothing is prefabricated. Every piece of cloth is cut and stitched together by hand, or by sewing machine. (Interesting note: there's at least one local sewing machine dealer who "Amishizes" sewing machines. He does this by removing the electrical systems and installing pedals for power.)

For Amish women, quilt making is both a practical endeavor and a means of socializing and expressing creativity. A "quilting bee" might be considered the Amish equivalent of a card party. Amish women gather for a day of sewing and socializing. Together, they create a quilt. Quilting is almost exclusively a female endeavor.

Amish women everywhere have been making quilts for a long time but the ones from Lancaster County have gained special recognition. They feature large, geometrical color fields while Midwestern Amish quilts have busier, patchwork patterns. Lancaster County quilts employ deep, rich colors, but no black. Black is common in the Midwest. And, Lancaster County quilts have distinct Amish designs while the Midwestern quilts frequently use traditional American designs. Two favorite Lancaster County designs are the "Diamond in the Square" and the "Center Square."

Lancaster County quilts are noteworthy for their central medallions and elaborate quilting. Often, it's necessary to look very closely to see the intricate sewing that has gone into making a quilt. Antique quilts were also unusual because they used no imagery—no houses, horses, etc. Today, quilt making is an important cottage industry for the Amish. The designs have changed slightly over the years, and the workmanship (workwomanship?) is still superb. Each quilt still requires a tremendous amount of work. Whatever the price may be, it doesn't come to much for each hour put into the quilt.

Often, quilts are donated to nonprofit organizations, such as fire companies and churches, and sold to raise funds.

Where to Look at Quilts: The **People's Place Quilt Museum** in Intercourse is home to the first permanent exhibit of antique Amish quilts. The Museum is on the second floor of the Old Country Store, Route 340 in Intercourse. Phone 717-768-7171.

Where to Buy Quilts: Finding quilts for sale is relatively easy. On highways and backroads, you'll see the "Quilts" sign. Prices tend to be a bit lower if you buy directly from the quilt maker.

Crafts

Amish and Mennonite craftspeople produce a wide variety of **dolls, furniture, wood carvings, toys, mailboxes,** and **pillows.** A distinctive feature of Amish dolls is that they have no faces. This is because of the Amish's interpretation of a biblical passage that warns against "graven images."

Hex Signs

On many barns in Pennsylvania Dutch Country, you'll see brightly colored signs designed to bring good luck—hex signs. They're circles with birds, stars, and flowers painted inside.

Over the years, many misconceptions about hex signs have developed. Hex signs are not Satanic, and they have no particularly deep symbolism. They're purely decorative.

Hex signs are also not Amish or Mennonite traditions. The Amish never place the signs on their barns. Lutherans and Reformed people who came to Pennsylvania at the invitation of William Penn introduced hex signs to the area. In fact, this

Hex signs.

is the only place in the world where the signs are hung on barns.

Antiques

Old things are big business in the Amish Country, although the antiques generally have no direct connection to the Amish. Antique dealers are common in the area and the small town of **Adamstown** on the Lancaster/Berks County line has gained recognition as the Sunday Antiques Capital of America. On Sundays, no fewer than eight antiques markets open their doors to dealers and the general public. Antiques of all descriptions and prices are available.

Occasionally, somebody makes an exceptionally lucky buy. In 1989, a man bought an unspectacular picture because he liked the frame. He paid four dollars. When he opened the frame, he found an original copy of the Declaration of Independence. That sold for well over a million dollars.

Bicycling

There's an old cliché about being in Rome and behaving as the Romans do. That theory can apply to a visit to the Amish Country. The best way to see the area is to travel as the natives do, which is slowly.

For visitors, bicycles can provide the best possible way to enjoy the Amish Country. On a bike, you'll move at a comfortable pace and you'll be much closer to everything. On a bike, it's easy to stop and take pictures, or to pull into a roadside stand. And, a bike puts some exercise into your vacation.

Vermont has long had a reputation as a bicycling utopia, but the Amish Country has everything that the Green Mountain State has, and more. And, although the Amish Country doesn't actually cover a lot of ground, you can ride for a long time before you'll start repeating yourself.

Many factors make the Amish Country quite popular with bicycling enthusiasts. One is that there are hundreds of miles of lightly travelled farm roads in the area. Lancaster County has more miles of road than any other county in Pennsylvania. Since the residents on many of those roads don't own cars, it's possible to ride for hours with minimal interference from internal-combustion-engine vehicles, and it's a simple matter to pull over and talk to the cows and horses. From the seat of a bike, you can also get a great view of the scenery.

Whether you're an experienced rider or not, you can easily find a ride that will suit your level of ability. There are areas of

(Courtesy Pennsylvania Dutch Visitors Bureau)

big hills, and flat sections. Many towns are close together. For instance, it's just about three miles from Intercourse to Paradise. On a leisurely two-hour ride, you can cover a lot of ground.

Where to Ride

The best piece of advice is to stay off the numbered highways. In their cars, visitors and local residents stick primarily to the major roads. There are, however, several major highways that are fairly decent for bikes. PA 340 and PA 741 east of Strasburg both have wide shoulders. Between Lancaster and Intercourse, 340 has a number of interesting stores and attractions. East of Strasburg, 741 is primarily farms.

The flattest part of the Amish Country is around Bird-In-Hand and Leola. This is also an area that's quite popular with bicyclists. The least congested part of the Amish Country lies south of Route 741, but that section is fairly hilly. The best times to ride are early in the morning, after 6 in the evening, and between 9 A.M. and 2 P.M.

Here are several rides. They're also good tours if you're in a car, but they're definitely better on a bike.

Bird-In-Hand

17 miles, easy terrain

Begin at Bird-In-Hand Farmer's Market on Route 340.
At west end of parking lot, go left on Maple Avenue.
Go right on South Ronks Road.
Go left on Irishtown Road. Be careful at train crossing. It's a high-speed Amtrak line.
Go left on Old Leacock Road.
Go over bridge and right on Vigilant Street.
Go left on East Gordon Road.
Go right on Belmont Road (covered bridge).
Go left on Harristown Road.
Go left on Frogtown Road.
Frogtown becomes Queen Road. Stay on Queen Road into Intercourse.

Go left on PA 772 West.

Merge into PA 340 West.

Stay on 340 back to Bird-In-Hand.

What You'll See: Many farms, a covered bridge, and attractions in Intercourse.

Strasburg
15 miles, moderate terrain

Begin at the Railroad Museum of Pennsylvania and go east on PA 741.

Go left on Paradise Lane.

Go right on Fairview Road.

Go right on Cherry Hill Road.

Go left on Oakhill Road.

Go right on Black Horse Road.

Go left on Quarry Road.

Go right on Belmont Road.*

Go right on PA 741 back to Strasburg.

Go right on White Oak Road.

Go right on Peach Lane.

Go left on Iva Road.

Go right on Rohrer Mill Road.

Cross PA 896.

Go left on 741 and back to Strasburg.

What You'll See: The Railroad Museum of Pennsylvania, the Strasburg Railroad, and many Amish farms.

*If you want to go farther and do some climbing, go straight on Belmont.

For the Strong of Quadriceps—The River Hills
30 miles, difficult terrain

Begin in Washington Boro, at the park at the intersection of Routes 441 and 999.

Go south on River Road.

Stay on River Road through Safe Harbor, past the Martic Forge Hotel, past Tucquan Glen, and until you come to Pinnacle Road.

Go right on Pinnacle Road. At the end of the road is the Holtwood Pinnacle, 537 feet above the Susquehanna River. It's a moderately spectacular view of the river.

From the Pinnacle, there's nothing to do but reverse your field. If you want to see some different sights, take a left on Bridge Valley Road. This will run you into the small town of Pequea. Then, go north on PA 324, back to River Road. If you want to ride through a covered bridge, make a right on Fox Hollow Road. The bridge is just off 324.

When you get back to Washington Boro, you'll realize that a mountain doesn't have to rise 5,000 or 10,000 feet to be long and steep.

What You'll See: Along River Road, you'll see woods and farms, but you won't see many flat sections. Most of the way, you'll be going up or down.

Biking Tips

In the Amish Country, bicyclists encounter several minor hazards that don't exist elsewhere:

1. Road apples. These are horses' way of letting you know they were there. You'll see them everywhere.

2. A rut worn in the road by horses' hooves. Generally, it's about a foot and a half out from the edge of the road. Be cautious of it—it could throw you. When you cross it, do so at an angle.

3. Oil and chipping. This is a primitive paving method still in use in Pennsylvania. Instead of using a conventional paving method, road crews will spray the road with oil and then cover it with small stone chips. Eventually, it smooths out, but if you come upon a section of road that has recently undergone this treatment, it can be quite annoying. It can also be dangerous if there are piles of stone. Sometimes, it's best just to avoid the section of road altogether, even if it means riding extra miles.

4. Crooked, narrow roads. Roads in the Amish Country rarely run straight. Going around the block may take you miles out of your way. These roads were in use long before cars existed. So, they're fine for bikes and buggies but tough for cars, buses, and trucks.

Despite these minor obstacles, biking in the Amish Country is an excellent way to see the area. If you don't have a bike, there are several bike touring companies. They'll supply you with everything you need for an enjoyable ride.

Lancaster Bicycle Touring, 3 Colt Ridge Lane, Strasburg, 717-786-4492.

New Horizons Bicycle Adventures, 3495 Horizon Drive, Lancaster, PA 17601, 717-285-7607.

If you're fairly adventurous, it's fun just to wander. Get yourself a road map and take off. A good slogan is, "Nowhere to go and all day to get there." In a day of wandering, you can cover a good chunk of the Amish Country. Be sure to take water, food, and a few dollars. In summer, it's also a good idea to carry a spoon, just in case you meet up with a cantaloupe or a watermelon.

If you enjoy group rides, the **Lancaster Bicycle Club** has them every week in good weather. Usually, they're on Saturdays and Sundays. When daylight permits, Wednesday evening rides are also included. For information on upcoming events, you can pick up a copy of the club newsletter at one of the bike shops, or you can call the club hot line at 717-396-9299 for a recorded message. The *Lancaster Sunday News* also lists the rides for the week in the Entertainment section.

Bike Shops

Bicycle World, 747 S. Broad Street, Lititz, 717-626-0650.

Bike Line, 117 Rohrerstown Road, Lancaster, 717-394-8998.

The Crank, Route 272, Ephrata, 717-733-8809.

Cycle Circle, 310 N. Queen Street, Lancaster, 717-295-3193.

Green Mountain Cyclery, 285fi S. Reading Road, Ephrata, 717-859-2422.

Lancaster Bicycle Shop, 1138 Manheim Pike, Lancaster, 717-299-9627.

Main Street Bikes, 301 E. Main Street, Lititz, 717-626-7490.

Martin's Bike Shop, Route 322, Hinkletown (east of Ephrata), 717-354-9127.

Active Recreation and Spectator Sports

There's no need to leave your fitness program at home when you come to the Amish Country. It's easy to get a workout into your vacation schedule. **Bicycling** through the Amish Country is an excellent way to combine travel and exercise. (See previous chapter.)

Runners usually find the scenery both enjoyable and different from what they left at home. Running is a good way to explore new surroundings. The weather in the Amish Country is quite conducive to year-round running. In summer, it can get uncomfortably hot in the middle of the day, but early mornings are always comfortable. In the dead of winter, middays are sometimes the best time for running.

Races

Road racing enthusiasts can find plenty of opportunities in the area. Some of the more popular races are:

Red Rose 5-Miler, first Saturday in June, downtown Lancaster.

Smith's Challenge 10K Trail Run (men only), Father's Day, Lancaster County Central Park.

Ephrata Firecracker 5-Miler, July 4.

Bowmansville Ox Trot, second Saturday in August.

Lancaster YMCA Triathlon, early September, Speedwell Forge Lake, north of lititz.

Conestoga Trail Run, 10 miles, late September, Pequea Creek Recreation Area.

Nissley Vineyards 7-Miler, first Saturday in October, Bainbridge.

Covered Bridge 10-Miler, late October, Atglen.

Swimming

The Lake at Mount Gretna, on PA 117 west of PA 72, is the area's favorite open water swimming spot. It's open Memorial Day to Labor Day. Call 717-964-3130 for details.

Lancaster County Central Park Pool, 1050 Rockford Road, Lancaster, 717-392-4621.

French Creek State Park, near Route 23 in Elverson, has pools and lakes. Call 215-582-9680 for hours and dates of operation.

Hiking

The Horseshoe Trail runs through Berks, Lebanon, and Lancaster counties. The best place to find it is in the **Middle Creek Wildlife Management Area,** on the lancaster/Lebanon County line. Middle Creek is home to thousands of ducks, geese, and other birds. In addition to the Horseshoe Trail, there are many miles of other hiking trails.

The area around **Lake Aldred,** in southern York and Lancaster counties, has almost 40 miles of hiking trails. Lake Aldred is actually a part of the Susquehanna River that's dammed up behind the Holtwood Dam. For information on the trails and other recreation opportunities in the area, contact Pennsylvania Power & Light Company's Holtwood Land Management Office at 717-284-2278.

Mount Gretna has many miles of wooded trails, including an abandoned railroad right-of-way, that are excellent for hiking and popular with runners. The railroad bed is flat. The other trails are pretty steep in many spots.

For a truly unusual hiking experience, try the unused roadbed in eastern Lancaster County known as **"the goat path,"** which was described in the Around the County chapter. A model airplane club uses a section as a landing strip. In some spots, cars drive through. And people walk on it.

To get to the goat path, take PA 23 west from Leola or east from Lancaster. Go south on Geist Road. At the *T* intersection, go right on Creek Hill Road, then left again on Geist. It's not far to the goat path.

Golf

For the golfing enthusiast, the Amish Country offers a variety of courses, from 9-hole, par-3 layouts to 18-hole courses. Several facilities combine lodging and golfing.

Crossgates Golf Club, 1 Crossland Pass, Millersville, 717-872-4500. New 18-hole course.

Evergreen Golf, Route 272, seven miles north of Lancaster, 717-898-7852. 18 hole par 3, pitch and putt. Also a short 18-hole, par-66 course.

Four Seasons, 949 Church Street, Landisville, 717-898-0104. Regulation 18-hole course. Also a pro shop and driving range.

Hawk Valley, 1319 Crestview Drive, Denver, 717-445-5445. 18-hole course, pro shop, and bed and breakfast.

Lancaster Host Resort, 2300 Lincoln Highway East, Lancaster, 717-299-5500 or 800-233-0121. Motel with 27 holes of golf, tennis courts, swimming pools, restaurants.

Overlook, 2040 Lititz Pike, Lancaster, 717-569-9551. Regulation 18-hole course, pro shop, and restaurant.

Rustic Meadows Camping & Golf Resort, 1980 Turnpike Road, Elizabethtown, 717-367-7718. Campgrounds with a 9-hole, par-3 course.

Tanglewood Manor, Scotland Road, Quarryville, 717-786-2220. Regulation 18-hole course.

Tree Top, Creek Road, Manheim, 717-665-6262. Regulation 18-hole course.

Willow Valley, Route 222/272, three miles south of Lancaster. 9-hole executive course, with motel, restaurants, swimming pools.

Places to Relax, Have a Picnic, Etc.

Chickies Rock County Park, Route 441, Columbia. Acres of semi-wilderness with trails and views of the Susquehanna River.

Ephrata Community Park, Oak Street, Ephrata. Home to The Playhouse in the Park and the Eicher Indian Museum, it's close to Main Street and the Ephrata Cloister.

Lancaster County Central Park, accessible from South Duke Street or Chesapeake Street in Lancaster. Approximately 560 acres, this park is home to Rock Ford Plantation, the home of Gen. Edward Hand. It also features miles of hiking/running trails, a covered bridge, an Exhibit Farm, the Garden of Five Senses, and plenty of places to have a picnic.

Lititz Springs Park, North Broad Street, Lititz. A shady escape right in the center of town. Ducks swim in the stream and special events are frequent.

Long's Park, Harrisburg Pike, Lancaster. Home of the world's largest chicken barbecue the third Saturday in May, Long's Park is next to Park City shopping mall. The amphitheater hosts musical performers and fireworks.

Mascot Park, at intersection of PA 772 and Stumptown Road, near Bird-In-Hand. It's small, but there are picnic tables and a stream. Across the road is Mascot Roller Mill.

Musser Park, 200 block of East Chestnut Street, downtown Lancaster. A tree-lined city park, with a major celebration on the Fourth of July.

New Holland Community Park, South Kinzer Avenue, New Holland. Home of the New Holland Band, it hosts many activities.

Northwest Corridor Park, 200 block of West Lemon Street, downtown Lancaster. About one-quarter of a mile long, this park was once a railroad bed. Now, it's a long and narrow park with a walking/biking trail, picnic benches, basketball courts, and playground equipment.

Paradise Memorial Park, Londonvale Road, Paradise. Just off Route 30, it's right beside the Pequea Creek.

Pequea Creek Recreation Area, Route 324, Pequea. A favorite place to watch the water flow by or to swim in it.

Safe Harbor Park, River Road, Safe Harbor. Close to the confluence of the Conestoga and Susquehanna rivers, the trees keep it pleasant on even the hottest days.

Susquehannock State Park, State Park Road, Drumore Township. Perched high above the Susquehanna River, it provides great views of the river and birds soaring on the breeze. There are also some rugged trails for adventurous hikers and runners.

Terre Hill Memorial Park, Lancaster Avenue, Terre Hill. On a clear day, you can get a great view of the Conestoga Valley.

Washington Boro Park, at intersection of PA 441 and PA 999. You can relax and watch the Susquehanna River roll by.

Spectator Sports

Once upon a time, many cities in Pennsylvania had **minor league baseball** teams. Today, Harrisburg and Reading have the only teams close to the Amish Country. Both are about 35 miles from downtown Lancaster.

The **major league** ball parks in Philadelphia and Baltimore are both about 65 miles from downtown Lancaster. In spite of the distances, local fans favor the Phillies over the Orioles by a significant margin. Many families were divided when the Orioles beat the Phillies in the 1983 World Series.

Penn National Race Course in Grantville runs thoroughbreds all year and is about 35 miles northwest of downtown Lancaster.

Hershey is home to the Hershey Bears minor league **hockey** team and the arena occasionally hosts **professional wrestling** and **college basketball.**

The Lehigh County Velodrome in Trexlertown is home to **bicycle racing** during the warm months. At certain times, the facility is open for use by anyone with a bicycle.

Below are some directions from Lancaster County:

Baltimore Orioles, 301-243-9800. Take U.S. 30 West to I-83 in York. Take 83 South to Baltimore and follow signs to stadium. Oriole Park is easily accessible from Pennsylvania. A light rail line from Timonium, on Route 83, goes directly to the stadium.

Harrisburg Senators, 717-231-4444. Take PA 283 west to I-283 North, then take I-83 South to Second Street (State Capitol) exit. Go north into Harrisburg. City Island Park is in the middle of the Susquehanna River.

Hershey Bears, 717-534-3911. Take PA 283 West to PA 743

North. Follow signs for HersheyPark Arena.

Lehigh County Velodrome, 215-965-6930. Take U.S. 222 North, through Reading to Trexlertown.

Penn National Race Course, 717-469-2211. Take PA 283 West to PA 743 North. Stay on 743 until it ends. Cross U.S. 22 and the racetrack is just ahead.

Philadelphia Phillies, Eagles, 76'ers, Flyers, Phillies 215-463-1000, Eagles 215-463-5500, 76'ers 215-339-7676, Flyers 215-755-9700. Take U.S. 30 East to PA 41. Go south on 41 to U.S. 1 North. Take U.S. 1 to U.S. 322 East. Take 322 East to I-95 North, which will take you to the stadium complex.

Reading Phillies, 215-375-8469. Take U.S. 222 North to Reading. Take PA 61 north to Reading Municipal Stadium.

Shopping

In the past decade, the Amish Country's fertile soil has begun to produce a new cash crop—shopping centers, especially outlet centers. Once, Reading (RED-ing) and surrounding Berks County made up the major outlet shopping region, but the number of outlets in Lancaster County has been growing rapidly.

As a rule, prices are lower in outlet stores than in conventional stores, but that's not always 100 percent true. By eliminating the middleman and selling directly to the public, manufacturers can keep prices lower.

In the outlet centers, you can buy almost anything—clothes, shoes, food, beauty aids, sporting goods, jewelry, umbrellas, rugs, tools, glassware, china, paper products, and much more. The outlets are so popular that they draw a steady tide of shoppers from points all over the East. Busloads of eager shoppers pour in almost daily.

Outlets aren't the only shopping attraction in the area, however. Many local craftsmen, including Amish men and women, produce and sell goods locally. And, there are many regular shopping centers and downtown stores.

Before the birth of shopping centers, downtown Lancaster was the place to shop. It still offers the best variety of stores, restaurants, and services. The Downtown Investment District has been doing an excellent job of revitalizing and promoting downtown shopping by keeping the area clean and marketing it with special events. During the holiday season, happenings such as Tuba Christmas draw shoppers and carolers downtown. On the first Friday night in December, Tuba Christmas brings together dozens of tuba players and singers to play Christmas carols and celebrate the lighting of a Christmas tree on Penn Square. From June through September, Night Out takes place on Wednesday nights from 6 to 9 P.M., bringing people downtown for entertainment, shopping, and dining. For shopping diversity, downtown Lancaster is the place to go.

Outlets

At these outlet centers, you'll find dozens of stores in one location. Compulsive shoppers might consider leaving the credit cards back at the hotel before venturing into an outlet mall. All outlet centers are open seven days a week.

Big Mill Factory Outlet Center, Eighth and Oley streets, Reading, 215-378-9100.

Manufacturers Outlet Mall (MOM), Exit 22 of PA Turnpike, Route 23, Morgantown, 215-286-2000. A shopping center of about 75 stores, with acres of parking and a hotel on the grounds.

9th Street Outlet Mart, 916 N. Ninth Street, Reading, 215-372-1144.

Reading Outlet Center, 801 N. Ninth Street, Reading, 215-375-5495.

Robesonia Outlet Center, Route 422, Robesonia, 215-693-3144.

VF Factory Outlet Complex, Hill Avenue and Park Road, Reading, 215-378-0408.

These centers are in the heart of the Amish Country:

Lancaster Outlet City, Route 30 east of Lancaster, 717-392-7202.

Quality Center, Route 30 and Route 896, Lancaster, 717-299-1949.

Rockvale Square, Route 30 and Route 896, Lancaster, 717-293-9595.

Individual Outlet Stores

Bollman Hat Outlet, Route 272 and Willow Street, Adamstown, 215-393-5251.

Lancaster Pottery & Glass, Route 30 East, Lancaster, 717-299-6835.

Loungewear Manufacturing, Route 322 east of Ephrata, 717-738-2026.

Susquehanna Glass Factory Store, Bird-In-Hand Farmer's Market, Route 340, 717-393-5670.

Totes Factory Outlet, 220 Centerville Road, Lancaster, 717-299-6526.

Van Heusen, 2811 Lincoln Highway East, Ronks, 717-687-0416.

Conventional Shopping Centers

East Towne Mall, Route 30 East, Lancaster, 717-394-6143.

Park City Center, Route 30 and Harrisburg Pike, west of Lancaster, 717-299-0010.

Shops Featuring Locally Made Items

Amishland Prints, corner of Routes 340 and 772 in Intercourse, 717-768-7273. Artist Xtian Newswanger produces prints of Amish people going about their daily lives.

Art Glassworks of Lancaster, 319 N. Queen Street, Lancaster, 717-394-4133. A working stained-glass studio offers custom work, supplies, and gifts.

Bird-In-Hand Bake Shop, 542 Gibbons Road, Bird-In-Hand, 717-656-7947. You'll find fresh baked goods and other treats here.

Community Creations, Brickerville House Courtyard, intersection of Routes 501 and 322, 717-627-2667; Manor West Commons, 2938 Columbia Avenue, Lancaster, 717-299-7064; Shoppes at Greenfield, 575 Greenfield Road, Lancaster, 717-396-0978. In three locations, these shops feature the works of local craftspeople, such as baskets, dolls, and pottery.

Country Barn Crafts, Route 340 just east of Bird-In-Hand. An

Amish family operates this shop in a refurbished barn. For sale are quilts, wall hangings, and Amish dolls.

Eldreth Pottery, 246 N. Decatur Street (Route 896), Strasburg, 717-687-8445. Salt-glazed stoneware is the specialty here. All pottery is handmade in Lancaster County, using traditional methods.

Jacob Zook's Hex & Craft Shops, Route 30 East, Paradise, 717-687-6333. Hex signs, the decorative displays on many barns, are the featured item here. Many craft items are also on display.

Kitchen Kettle Village, Route 340, Intercourse, 717-768-8261. A collection of 30 shops where crafts and foods are created.

Little Red Wagons, Mondale Road, Bird-In-Hand, 717-656-9605. Lapp Welding produces the little red wagons that have been a part of many childhoods. The shop is within a mile of two covered bridges.

Martin's Chair Shop, 124 King Court, New Holland, PA 17557, 717-355-2177. Lancaster County craftsmen produce chairs and other wooden furniture.

Miller's Natural Foods, Monterey Road, Bird-In-Hand. A health food store on an Amish farm offers as big a selection as a store in a mall, with prices low enough to make it worthwhile for people from Maryland and Delaware to drive the extra distance. Miller's own bread and produce are usually available.

The Old Candle Barn, Route 30, Intercourse, 717-768-3231. Amish artists carve and dip candles on the premises.

The Old Country Store, Main Street, Intercourse, 717-768-7101. A collection of quilts and crafts from Amish and Mennonite craftspeople.

Old Road Furniture Company, Main Street (Route 340), Intercourse, 717-768-7171. Amish craftsmen create tables, desks, and chests. Also available are reproductions of antique Amish quilts, wall hangings, and dolls.

Olde Millhouse Shoppes, 105 Strasburg Pike, Lancaster, 717-299-0678. Located in an old barn, this store provides many items that create a country look—furniture, lamps, folk art, and decorations.

Petersheim's Quilt Shop, 207 N. Harvest Road, Bird-In-Hand. See quilts made by an Amish woman and buy them directly.

The Saltbox, 3004 Columbia Avenue, Lancaster, 717-392-5649. Using tin and brass, craftsmen create reproductions of lighting fixtures used in colonial times.

SelfHelp Crafts of the World, 240 N. Reading Road (PA 272), Ephrata, 717-738-1101. The Mennonite Church sells crafts from many countries around the world and returns the profits to the people who created the items.

Will-Char Hex Shop, Route 30 East, Paradise, 717-687-8329. Hex signs, weather vanes, lawn ornaments, and handwoven rugs are on display in this A-frame building.

Witmer Quilt Shop, 1070 W. Main Street (Route 23), New Holland, 717-656-3911. This in-home store features several rooms where the quilts are piled high on the beds.

Other Interesting Shops

Basketville, Route 30, Paradise, 717-442-9444. Baskets of many descriptions are on display here.

Donecker's, 409 N. State Street, Ephrata, 717-733-2231. Fashion stores for men and women, with fashion shows almost every day. Close to the Restaurant at Donecker's, Donecker's Guesthouse, and Donecker's Artworks.

Krafts & Kollectors, 2400 Lincoln Highway East, 717-394-6404. A large collection of mugs, mirrors, bottles, steins, and clocks.

Moore Bears, Route 896 at Hershey Farm, Strasburg, 717-687-6954. A huge collection of teddy bears, with personalized bears a specialty.

Stoltzfus Woodworking Shop, PA 772 between Monterey and Mascot, south of PA 23, 717-646-6719 between 6 and 8 A.M. Manufacturers of storage sheds, furniture, and picnic tables.

Strasburg Country Store & Creamery, on the square in Strasburg, 717-687-0766. A favorite place to stop for ice cream, especially after a ride on the Strasburg Railroad.

Teddy Bear Emporium, 51 N. Broad Street (PA 501), Lititz, 717-626-8334. Thousands of teddy bears and plush toys.

Entertainment/ Night Life

No one will ever mistake the Amish Country for Broadway, but there is a good variety of entertainment available. Plays, movies, concerts, and even tractor pulls happen regularly. Local papers give weekly listings of what's going on. Several weekly and monthly publications are distributed free in motels, restaurants, and information centers.

Buck Motorsports Park, PA 272 south of Lancaster, 717-859-4244 or 717-284-2139. Presents a form of racing that you won't see everywhere. Farm tractors and four-wheel-drive trucks race each other. They're not the kind of tractors that you'll see on farms, though. Some of these monstrosities can generate up to 3,000 horsepower.

Chameleon, 223 N. Water Street, Lancaster, 717-393-7133. Has live bands and dancing.

Dutch Apple Dinner Theater, 510 Centerville Road, at Centerville Road exit of Route 30 bypass, 717-898-1900. Dutch Apple offers dining to complement professionally produced musicals and comedies throughout the year.

Dutch Wonderland Amusement Park, 2249 Route 30 East of Lancaster, 717-291-1888. Has rides, botanical gardens, food, gift shops, and everything else that you'd expect to find in an amusement park.

Ephrata Star Playhouse in the Park, Ephrata Park, 717-733-7966. Offers fine summer theater.

Fulton Opera House, 12 N. Prince Street, Lancaster, 717-397-

7425. Offers plays and concerts, featuring both local and New York actors and actresses throughout the year. The building itself is a National Historic Landmark, built in 1852.

Green Room Theater at Franklin and Marshall College, College Avenue, Lancaster, 717-291-4015. Presents shows during the academic year.

Hershey Theater, 15 E. Caracas Avenue, Hershey, 717-534-3405. Presents Broadway shows, dances, etc., throughout the year.

HersheyPark, Hershey, 800-HERSHEY. Has roller coasters, food, the Kissing Tower, and much more.

Mount Hope Estate and Winery, Route 72 North of Manheim, at the PA Turnpike exit, 717-665-7285. Produces the Renaissance Faire, a celebration of life in medieval England, on weekends from late June through October.

Music at Gretna, Mount Gretna Playhouse, Box 519, Mount Gretna, PA 17604, 717-964-3836. Presents a summer series of chamber music—jazz, string quartets, pianists, etc. During the winter of 1994, snow collapsed the playhouse, so the performers have had to find other facilities. Call ahead for information.

Rainbow Dinner Theater, Revere Tavern, Route 30, Paradise, 717-299-4300. Presents matinee dinner shows.

Timbers Dinner Theater in Mount Gretna, 717-964-3601. Shows and dining.

Villa East Comedy Club, 2231 Lincoln Highway East, Lancaster, 717-397-4973. Stand-up comedians and dining.

Village Nightclub, 205 N. Christian Street, Lancaster, 717-397-5000. Offers live bands and dancing.

Movie Theaters

Columbia Drive-In, Route 462, Columbia, 717-684-0621. The last drive-in still operating in Lancaster County.

Eden Twin, Oregon Pike and Route 30, Lancaster, 717-569-1770.

Eric Pacific 4, 237 N. Queen Street, Lancaster, 717-397-6151.

Eric Twin, Brunswick Mall, Lancaster, 717-394-8481.

Kendig Square Movies, Kendig Square Shopping Center, Willow Street, 717-464-2994.

Manor Cinemas, Manor Shopping Center, Millersville Pike, Lancaster, 717-399-3300 or 399-3301.

Wonderland 4, Route 30 East, Lancaster, 717-394-7251.

Special Events

These are annual events, but their dates of operation can change from year to year.

Farm Fairs

One of the major traditions in rural areas is the fair. In Lancaster County, fairs are still big social events. They're an interesting mix of agricultural exhibits, rides, carnival games, parades, and food. Farm fairs generally last four or five days and some of them involve the entire town. In Ephrata and New Holland, for instance, the main streets through town are closed off for the fairs. The parade is one of the major events in town. Local residents stake out spots days in advance to guarantee themselves good seats for the marching bands and floats.

At the fair, there are contests for just about everything. Livestock, fruits, vegetables, quilts, paintings, canned goods, and baked goods win ribbons for their owners. Everybody has a chance to win something.

Fair season lasts for about six weeks from late August to early October. The local papers always run stories heralding the beginning of Fair Season. Elizabethtown, in the western end of Lancaster County, hosts the season's first fair. Others are in Lampeter, Quarryville, Manheim, Denver, Ephrata, and New Holland. If you want to get a real glimpse of rural/small-town Lancaster County, get to a farm fair.

Corn Roasts, Pancake Breakfasts, Church Suppers, Etc.

If you look at the message boards outside churches and fire-halls, you'll almost certainly see notices for various eating events. These are fund raisers and social gatherings, and they're usually open to everyone. In true Amish Country tradition, your admission fee will normally buy all that you can eat.

These food fests take place all year, and they're listed in the local papers. On just about any weekend, a church or a fire company will be having a breakfast or a supper. If you want to enjoy some real local cooking, stop in.

According to its organizers, the **Sertoma Club's chicken barbecue** is the world's largest. It takes place on the third Saturday in May at Long's Park in Lancaster, right beside Park City Center. For several days, Sertoma members build pits to roast the chickens. On Saturday, they barbecue thousands of birds. The proceeds from the event help to maintain the park.

Auctions

Another popular way to raise funds is to have an auction. Many fire companies and church groups have auctions. They sell anything and everything. If you come to one of these auctions, you may find antique quilts, or old bottles, and everything in between. These auctions are extremely popular, drawing potential buyers from miles away.

One of the biggest and most famous of the auctions is the **Gordonville Fire Company Auction,** held in early March. It's become a tradition. Local residents donate quilts, and just about everything else, to benefit the fire company. This fire company also hosts a quilt sale and a buggy auction. For details, call 717-768-3869.

Public sales are also a popular local tradition. These frequently take place when someone dies and the relatives want to sell the belongings. At public sales, houses, cars, and other personal belongings go to the highest bidder. In Lancaster County, public sales are big events. It's not unusual for hundreds of potential buyers to show up, and usually someone is

Leola Produce Auction.

selling refreshments. To find out where the public sales are, check the classified pages of the local papers.

There are some auctions that take place on a more regular basis. At the **Leola Produce Auction,** on Brethren Church Road, local farmers sell off their produce. It can be a fascinating sight, as Amish and Mennonite farmers bring horse-drawn wagons filled with corn, melons, tomatoes, and many other produce items to market. The only drawback is that it's not designed to present buying opportunities for individuals, unless you're in the mood for 100 dozen ears of corn or 200 cantaloupes. Most buyers are from supermarkets, and the quantities are more than an individual or a family could handle. The Produce Auction opens in spring and operates through autumn. To find out the days of the week when it's open, call 717-656-9592.

Martin Auctioneers, at the intersection of PA 340 and New Holland Road, east of Intercourse, regularly hosts various types of auctions. A big one is the annual sale of antique carriages, coaches, and sleighs. The auction draws buyers from many states. Martin's phone is 717-768-8108.

The **Farmersville Auction,** east of Brownstown on Farmersville Road, sells furniture and household goods to the highest bidders. The phone is 717-354-5095.

Root's Market, Route 72 North of East Petersburg (open Tuesdays), and **Green Dragon Market,** Route 272 North of Ephrata (open Fridays), both have auctions of various types of goods. Frequently they're closeouts or goods with minor damage, but the merchandise is always functional, and the prices are lower than they'd be in a store.

Calendar

Every month has much to offer the visitor. The warmer months offer more attractions, fairs, etc. In keeping with rural tradition, the harvest months of September and October are filled with fairs and various celebrations.

January

Pork and Sauerkraut Dinner, New Year's Day, Leola Fire Company, Route 23, Leola.

Pennsylvania Farm Show, second week of month, Harrisburg. The biggest display of the state's agricultural bounty. Tradition says that the worst weather of the year always comes during Farm Show week.

February

Ground Hog Day, February 2. Tradition says that Octorara Orphie will emerge from his burrow and predict whether the next six weeks will be mild or harsh.

Fasnacht Day, Tuesday before first day of Lent. Bakeries throughout the Dutch Country produce fasnachts (doughnuts) as a final splurge before the self-denial of the Lenten season. Fasnachts are available at markets and in stores and restaurants throughout the area.

March

Gordonville Fire Company Auction, second Saturday, 717-

768-3869. It's the largest fireman's auction on the East Coast. Quilts, handcrafts, and farm equipment all sold to raise money for the volunteer fire company.

Charter Day for State Museums, second Sunday. Offers free admission to Cornwall Iron Furnace, Ephrata Cloister, Landis Valley Museum, and Railroad Museum of Pennsylvania.

Spring Fever 10K Run, fourth Saturday, Middle Creek Wildlife Preserve.

Philadelphia Flower Show, Civic Center, 215-625-8250.

Spring planting begins.

April

Quilters Heritage Celebration, Thursday through Sunday after first Monday of month, Sheraton Lancaster Golf Resort, 717-299-5500. A collection of quilts, quilters, and quilt-making equipment and fabrics.

Earth Day Fair, third Friday, downtown Lancaster.

Sheep Shearing, last Thursday and Friday, Amish Farm & House, Lancaster, 717-394-6185.

Art Walk, last weekend, downtown Lancaster.

Spring planting continues.

May

Loyalty Day Parade, first Saturday, downtown Lancaster.

Lancaster Spring Show of Arts & Crafts, first weekend, Lancaster County Central Park, 717-295-1500.

Spring Steam-Up, second weekend, Rough and Tumble Museum, Kinzers, 717-442-4249.

Opening Day, second weekend, HersheyPark, 800-HERSHEY.

Rhubarb Festival, third Saturday, Kitchen Kettle Village, Intercourse, 800-732-3538.

World's largest chicken barbecue, third Saturday, Long's Park, Lancaster.

Riverside Craft Days, Memorial Day weekend, John Wright Mansion, Wrightsville, 717-252-2519.

Bicycle Races, citizens' and semipro races the Sunday before Memorial Day, CoreStates International 90-mile race for serious professionals the Tuesday after Memorial Day, downtown Lancaster.

Strawberry picking begins, late in month.

June

Red Rose 5-Mile Run, first Saturday, downtown Lancaster.

Landis Valley Fair, first weekend, Landis Valley Farm Museum, 717-569-0401.

Woodcarving Show, first Saturday, Kitchen Kettle Village, Intercourse, 800-732-3538.

Run For Peace 10K, second Saturday, Lititz Church of the Brethren.

Smith's Challenge 10K and 20K Trail Run, Father's Day, Lancaster County Central Park.

Kutztown Folk Festival, last weekend in June through first week of July, 215-683-8707. A huge celebration of Pennsylvania Dutch culture, music, and food.

The first local corn and tomatoes reach market, late in month.

July

Civil War Re-enactment, weekend preceding July 4, Gettysburg Battlefield.

Patriotic Concerts and Fireworks, July 3, Lancaster.

Old Fashioned Fourth, July 4, Musser Park, Lancaster, 717-393-1133.

Firecracker 5 Mile footrace, July 4, Ephrata.

Music in the Vineyards, Saturday evenings, July through Labor Day, Nissley Winery, Bainbridge, 717-426-3514.

Bavarian Summer Festival, mid-July through Labor Day, Stoudt's Black Angus, Adamstown, 215-484-4385.

Art Show, third Saturday, Kitchen Kettle Village, Intercourse, 800-732-3538.

Ice Cream Festival, third Sunday, downtown Lancaster.

Pennsylvania State Craft Show & Sale, last Thursday through Sunday, Franklin and Marshall College, Lancaster.

Terre Hill Days, last or next-to-last Saturday. Town festival and five-mile race.

Lititz Outdoor Art Show, last Saturday, downtown Lititz, 717-738-0627.

August

Annual Bridge Bust, first Saturday, Route 462 bridge between Columbia and Wrightsville, 717-684-5249. For one day, this mile-long bridge is closed to motor vehicles and opened for food, crafts, etc.

Fiddler's Picnic, first Sunday, Lancaster County Central Park, 717-299-8215.

Lebanon Bologna Festival, second weekend, Lebanon County Fairgrounds, 717-272-8555.

Lancaster Fest, second Saturday, downtown Lancaster. Street fair and celebration of cultures.

Heritage Day, second Saturday, Hans Herr House, Willow Street, 717-464-4438.

Long's Park Day of Music, second Sunday, Lancaster.

Old Thresherman's Reunion, middle of month, Rough and Tumble Museum, Kinzers, 717-442-4249.

Lost Dutchman Gemboree, third week, Historic Strasburg Inn, 717-392-6825. A festival featuring gems, minerals, and fossils from all over the world.

Elizabethtown Fair, begins third Wednesday of month, 717-367-7256. The first agricultural fair in Lancaster County.

Covered Bridge Metric Century Bike Ride, third Sunday, Greenfield Corporate Center, Lancaster. This 100K ride takes riders through seven of Lancaster County's covered bridges. Call Lancaster Bicycle Club, 717-396-9299.

Mount Gretna Outdoor Art Show, third weekend.

Pennsylvania Renaissance Faire, begins last weekend in August and runs through October, Mount Hope Estate, Route 72 and PA Turnpike, 717-665-7021.

September

Arts & Crafts Festival, Labor Day weekend, Long's Park, Lancaster, 717-295-7001.

Lancaster YMCA Triathlon/Duathlon, weekend after Labor Day, Speedwell Forge Lake, 717-397-7474.

Mill Bridge Village "Family" Octoberfest, weekends in September and October, Mill Bridge Village, Strasburg, 717-687-6521.

Denver Community Fair, second week, Denver Memorial Park, 215-267-2931.

Quilt Auction, midmonth, Gordonville Fire Company, 717-768-3869.

Craft Fair, second Saturday, Plain & Fancy Farm, Bird-In-Hand, 717-768-8281.

Solanco Agricultural Fair, third Thursday through Saturday, Quarryville, 717-786-1054.

Harvest Festival, third Saturday, Kitchen Kettle Village, Intercourse, 800-732-3538.

Ephrata Agricultural Fair, last week of month, Ephrata, 717-733-2425.

West Lampeter Community Fair, last Thursday through Saturday, Lampeter, 717-464-2270.

Fall Antique Extravaganza, last weekend, Stoudt's Black Angus, Adamstown, 215-484-4385.

October

Harvest Days, first weekend, Landis Valley Museum, Lancaster, 717-569-0401. The apple is king at this re-creation of early Pennsylvania harvest days. Cider and apple pies are made on the grounds. There are demonstrations of blacksmithing, quilting, and gardening techniques.

Nissley Vineyards Seven-Mile Race, first Saturday, 717-426-3514.

New Holland Farmer's Fair, first week, New Holland, 717-354-8921.

Art Sunday, first Sunday, downtown Lancaster.

Snitz Festival, second Saturday, Hans Herr House, Willow Street, 717-464-4438. Apples dominate this celebration of early Pennsylvania life.

A Time of Harvest, second weekend, Rough and Tumble Museum, Kinzers, 717-442-4249. Harvest celebration features cider and harvest activities.

Fall Jazz Festival and Outdoor Art Show, Sunday before Columbus Day, downtown Lancaster.

Manheim Community Fair, second week, 717-664-3710.

Pretzel Twist 5-Mile Run, third Saturday, Lititz.

Town Fair, fourth Tuesday and Wednesday, downtown Lancaster. Arts and crafts exhibits.

Edgar Allan Poe Celebration, weekends around Halloween, Mount Hope Estate, Route 72 and PA Turnpike, 717-665-7021.

Halloween Ghost Trains, weekends around Halloween, Strasburg Railroad, 717-687-7522.

Halloween Lantern Tours, weekends around Halloween, Railroad Museum of Pennsylvania, Strasburg, 717-687-8628.

November

Harrisburg Marathon, second Sunday, downtown Harrisburg.

Christmas in Hershey, midmonth through December, 800-HERSHEY.

Jack Frost Parade, Saturday before Thanksgiving, downtown Lancaster.

A Charles Dickens Christmas Past, weekends late November through December, Mount Hope Estate, Route 72 and PA Turnpike, 717-665-7021.

Savor the Season, late November through December, Kitchen Kettle Village, Intercourse, 800-732-3538.

Christkindlesmarkt, Sundays in late November and December, Stoudt's Black Angus, Adamstown, 215-484-4385.

December

Tuba Christmas, first Friday evening in downtown Lancaster. Carolers sing to the accompaniment of dozens of tubas.

Old-Fashioned Holiday Weekends, first three weekends, downtown Lancaster, 717-399-7977.

Victorian Christmas, early in month, James Buchanan's

Christmas Candlelight Tours, first weekend, Hans Herr House, Willow Street, 717-464-4438. A demonstration of colonial Mennonite life, including caroling around a bonfire.

Annual Christmas Cantata, first weekend, Lancaster Bible College, 717-569-7071. Cantata with brass, organ, and piano accompaniment.

Holiday Candlelight Tours, first weekend, Rock Ford Plantation, Lancaster, 717-392-7223.

Jingle Bell Run (5K race) and Fire Engine Parade, second Sunday, downtown Lancaster.

A Christmas Evening at Landis Valley, third Tuesday, 717-569-0401. Music, refreshments, and Pennsylvania German Christmas trees.

Countdown Lancaster, New Year's Eve, downtown Lancaster.

Places Nearby

While the Amish Country has enough to keep you occupied, there are some places worth seeing nearby. Within an hour's drive of Lancaster County, you'll find the site of the bloodiest battle in the history of North America, Chocolatetown, U.S.A., and the capital of Pennsylvania. A little farther away are Philadelphia, Baltimore, and the Pocono Mountains.

Gettysburg

Gettysburg gained lasting fame from July 1 to July 3, 1863 when Union and Confederate soldiers battled each other in and around the small town. Today, Gettysburg is still a small town and it derives much of its income from tourism. The battlefield itself is preserved in **Gettysburg National Military Park** and it remains largely as it was when the fighting stopped.

In late June and during the first week in July, **Civil War Heritage Days** commemorate the Battle of Gettysburg with an encampment, lectures, and a battle re-enactment.

The battlefield is a beautiful place all year and it's especially scenic in late April and early May, when the dogwood trees are in bloom. For information on Gettysburg, call the Gettysburg Travel Council at 717-334-6274.

To reach Gettysburg from Lancaster County, just follow Route 30 West. It's about 50 miles from downtown Lancaster.

Hershey

Hershey, sometimes known as Chocolatetown, U.S.A., is home to **Hershey Foods, HersheyPark,** and **HersheyPark Stadium.**

Hershey Foods makes the famous Hershey chocolate bar and many other foods. HersheyPark is a place for summer fun. The large amusement park has many rides. The most famous is the Superdooperlooper. HersheyPark Stadium brings in big-name entertainers. Whitney Houston, Gloria Estefan, Don Henley, and Poison have appeared here. Big shows for 1995 included the Ice Capades, singer John Anderson, and the Mighty Morphin Power Rangers.

Hershey is also home to **Milton Hershey School.** Milton Hershey, the man behind the candy bar and the park, started the school to care for needy children. On the campus is Founder's Hall, a monument to the man and his wife.

For information on Hershey, call 800-HERSHEY.

To get to Hershey from Lancaster County, take PA 283 West to PA 743 North. You can also reach Hershey by following U.S. 322 West. Once you get to Hershey, signs will point you in the right directions.

Harrisburg

Harrisburg is the capital of Pennsylvania. The **Capitol Building** is an impressive edifice. The **Harrisburg Senators** minor league baseball team plays on City Island, which is in the middle of the Susquehanna River. The **State Museum of Pennsylvania** has exhibits on the history, geology, industry, and arts of Pennsylvania.

To reach Harrisburg from Lancaster, follow PA 283 West to I-283 North. Then take I-83 into the city. Exit at Second Street, the last exit before the Susquehanna River.

Millersburg

For a different way to cross the river, follow PA 147 North to Millersburg. There, you'll find the **Millersburg Ferry.** Running between Millersburg and the west shore near Liverpool, it takes about 20 minutes to cross. The ferry isn't a tourist attraction. There are no bridges across the river from Duncannon to Sunbury. For information, call 717-444-3200.

Reading

Reading has long enjoyed a reputation as a place to go for **bargain shopping.** The outlet stores attract shoppers from great distances. They can buy clothes, sporting goods, shoes, and many more kinds of items in the large warehouse buildings that house the outlet shops. Reading is off U.S. 222 and U.S. 422.

Philadelphia

Philadelphia and Lancaster started out growing up together. The first turnpike in the country linked the two cities. Eventually, Philadelphia grew much larger than Lancaster, and became decidedly urban while Lancaster and surrounding areas retained a rural flavor.

In a car, it's easy to get to Philadelphia from anywhere in the Amish Country. By train, it's even easier. Amtrak runs frequently between Lancaster and 30th Street Station in Philadelphia. For complete information on Philadelphia, get *A Marmac Guide to Philadelphia,* published by Pelican Publishing Company.

Baltimore

Baltimore is a city that has enjoyed a revitalization in recent years. The **Inner Harbor** attracts visitors for food and shopping. **Oriole Park,** the new baseball stadium, is a re-creation of ball parks built at the turn of the century, with asymmetrical dimensions, a grass field, and seats close to the playing field. It's a nice place when players aren't on strike. Baltimore was the home of Babe Ruth and Edgar Allan Poe. Francis Scott Key wrote "The Star Spangled Banner" in Baltimore.

The easiest way to get to Baltimore is to take U.S. 30 West to I-83 South at York. Traveling tip: you'll save time and miles by going left at the first traffic light on Route 30 in York. At the intersection with PA 462, go right and directly onto the ramp to I-83 South. A more scenic route is to take U.S. 222 South to U.S. 1 South, which runs right into Baltimore.

Coal Country

While farming was becoming the dominant industry in southeastern Pennsylvania, coal was bringing prosperity to much of the rest of the state. Large parts of the state were known as "the coal regions." Many towns developed as company towns.

Today, some coal mining still goes on in Pennsylvania, surprisingly close to the Amish Country.

At the **Anthracite Museum of Ashland** (Schuylkill County), 717-875-4708, you can see exhibits of coal-mining techniques and equipment, and you can take a ride inside a real coal mine.

At **Eckley Miner's Village,** east of Hazelton (Luzerne County), 717-636-2070, you'll find a 19th-century mining town.

In Centralia, Columbia County, an underground mine fire has been burning for years. It's basically destroyed the town, forcing most people to leave their homes.

The coal regions run roughly from Lykens in northern Dauphin County, northeast to Scranton.

Trivia

—From 1760 to 1810, Lancaster was the largest inland city in the United States.

—Pennsylvania's only president, James Buchanan, was from Lancaster. His home, Wheatland, is just west of the city line on Route 23 (Marietta Avenue).

—Lancaster County has more miles of roads than any other county in Pennsylvania.

—The Strasburg Railroad is the oldest short line railroad in the country.

—The longest covered bridge ever built, 5,690 feet, spanned the Susquehanna River at Columbia. Union soldiers burned it to cut off the Confederates during the Civil War.

—The first commercial telegraph line operated between Lancaster and Harrisburg in 1846.

—Benjamin Franklin was one of the major patrons of Franklin College, which in 1853 merged with Marshall College to become Franklin and Marshall College, now on College Avenue in Lancaster.

—Local legend says that "wooly bears"—caterpillars—are good predictors of the coming winter's severity. According to the legend, the more black a caterpillar has, the worse the winter will be.

—At one time, Mill Creek had 12 mills on it.

—The nation's first turnpike, from Philadelphia to Lancaster, was completed in 1794.

—Robert Fulton, the first man to make navigation by steam practical, was born in southern Lancaster County.

—William Henry, the first man to suggest powering boats by steam, was a Lancastrian.

—The Conestoga wagon originated in Lancaster County.

—Thaddeus Stevens, a congressman from Lancaster, was so popular that he was re-elected after his death in 1868.

—After his first store failed in Utica, N.Y., F. W. Woolworth established his first successful five and ten in Lancaster in 1879. It was at the southwest corner of Queen and Chestnut streets. Today, a Woolworth's store is a block and a half south on Queen Street.

—Sturgis Pretzels in Lititz is widely considered the first pretzel house in the country.

—Reading calls itself "Pretzel City."

—A mine in eastern Lancaster County was the only nickel mine in North America from 1855 to 1885. There's still a Nickel Mines Road.

—Milton Hershey, of chocolate fame, made his first chocolate bars in Lancaster.

—The world's largest chicken barbecue takes place the third Saturday of May at Long's Park in Lancaster.

—Lancaster County is the most productive, non-irrigated farm county in the U.S.

—Lancaster County has the largest Mennonite community in the world and the second largest (behind Holmes County, Ohio) Amish community in the world.